Get Lucky Now!

Get Lucky Now!

The Seven Secrets For Abundant Health, Wealth, And Happiness

Dr. Stephen Simpson

Copyright © 2016 Dr. Stephen Simpson
All rights reserved.

ISBN-13: 9781515398684
ISBN-10: 1515398684
Library of Congress Control Number: 2015913672
CreateSpace Independent Publishing Platform
North Charleston, South Carolina

Table of Contents

Preface · ix
Introduction · xiii
      Ten Months into My Get-Lucky-Now
      Project—November 2014 · xiv
      I Blame the Drugs · xvi
      Time to Put on Your Party Clothes and Celebrate · · · · · · · xix
      If You Can't Beat Them, Join Them · · · · · · · · · · · · · · · · xxi
      When All Else Fails, Read the Instructions · · · · · · · · · · · xxii
      A Color TV Will Always Be Better Than
      a Black-and-White One · xxiii
      Meditation Booth · xxv

Chapter 1 Goals · 1
      Self-Knowledge · 3
      How to Choose a Wonderful Goal · · · · · · · · · · · · · · · · · 5
      Bring Life to Your Goal · 7
      The Ultimate Goal Is Not to Have One · · · · · · · · · · · · · · · 9
      Meditation Booth · 10
Chapter 2 Confidence · 11
      Internal Dialogue · 12
      Remember the Good Times · 13
      Look Like You Feel and Feel Like You Look · · · · · · · · · · · · 14
      Meditation Booth · 16

Chapter 3	Visualization · 17
	Make Sense of Your Five Senses and
	Go Large with Your Movie · 20
	Meditation Booth · 22
Chapter 4	Mindfulness · 23
	The Tip of the Iceberg · 23
	House of Cards · 25
	Back to Nature · 26
	Can't Live with Them, Can't Live without Them · · · · · · · · · 27
	Why Don't You Listen to What I Say? · · · · · · · · · · · · · · 28
	Keep It Simple · 30
	Give Your Brain a Holiday · · · · · · · · · · · · · · · · · · · 31
	Meditation Booth · 32
Chapter 5	The 3 Hs Of Havening, Heartmath, And Hypnosis · · · · · · · 33
	Finding a Safe Place · 34
	Self-Havening Instructions · · · · · · · · · · · · · · · · · · · 37
	Finding a Coherent Place · · · · · · · · · · · · · · · · · · · 38
	Finding a Deep Place · 42
	Meditation Booth · 46
Chapter 6	The Luck Magnet · 47
	You Do Not Need to Spend Ten Years in
	Day Jail, Though It Helps · · · · · · · · · · · · · · · · · · · 47
	Do as They Do · 48
	Good Luck or Bad Luck? · 50
	When the Going Gets Tough, the Tough Get Going · · · · · · 52
	It Is Good to Be Nice, But Not Too Nice · · · · · · · · · · · 53
	Meditation Booth · 55
Chapter 7	Magic · 56
	This Is the Answer · 57
	All in Good Time · 58
	Yet More Rules · 59
	Show Me the Money · 60
	There Is Nothing to Worry About · · · · · · · · · · · · · · · · 63

  Who Let the Cat Out? ·64
  Meditation Booth ·67

Conclusion ·69
  What Next? ·69
  Run with the Ball ·70
About the Author ·73
Notes ·75

Preface

I AM STEPHEN SIMPSON, a medical doctor and fellow of the Royal Society of Medicine. I have worked exclusively as an elite performance director for the last seven years. My role as a mind coach is to help my clients operate at their peak performance level more consistently. We achieve this together by using proven psychological techniques that unlock the latent power of their unconscious minds. On occasions these techniques may even ignite skills that they did not know they possessed, leading to significantly accelerated progress toward their desired results.

I appear regularly on TV and radio, and my clients include leading names from the diverse worlds of sports, business, the entertainment industries, and professional poker.

I am also a best-selling author and presenter, as well as a feature writer for *The Best You* magazine. My articles are published in leading newspapers and magazines.

I am sharing this glitzy introduction with you not to massage my ego, but for a far more important reason. Let me ask you a question.

Would you hire a financial advisor who has difficulty meeting mortgage payments?

Would you consult with a life coach who has serious, unresolved personal issues?

Would you be prepared to make significant life changes to achieve abundant health, wealth, and happiness on the basis of recommendations from a person who has not experienced abundant health, wealth, and happiness?

Of course you would not. So now you will understand why I shared just a few details of my life with you.

The seeds for this book were planted in January 2014. Like many other people, I always start each year with a cunning plan.

My plan for 2014 was to devote more time and energy into presenting self-development workshops. I enjoy the challenge of thinking on my feet and exchanging views with delegates from diverse backgrounds. I get a real kick from watching them as they ignite skills they did not know they possessed. It is fun being a catalyst, not doing very much apart from facilitating them to get out of their own way and find the flow.

My cunning plan turned out to be far from that. Although there have been many other speaking engagements, there have been no workshops, other than a single event in London in January 2014. That is because something very exciting happened there.

I planned to talk about success and how we could learn from successful people to create more success in our lives, too. I never use scripts but instead trust that the right words will surface. Sometimes this works well while other times it leads to surprises, as it did this time. I asked the delegates if they wanted to be healthier, wealthier, and happier this year. Not surprisingly, they all agreed. Then my brain and mouth disconnected, and I asked a question that was not in the running order.

The question was this: "Do you want to be lucky this year?"

I surprised myself with this question, and the delegates' reaction surprised me even more. A tangible ripple passed through the audience. The delegates leaned forward intently. It was as if time had stopped—no movement, no sound, and my mouth had stopped working, too. I had goose bumps.

I did not understand what had happened, but I knew that one single word, "luck," had just deeply resonated in the reptilian part of everyone's brains. I knew that our single most important desire this year was to be lucky. And I knew that my cunning plan had been replaced with a totally different one.

The new plan was to explore luck and fathom why some people have more of it than others and how we can get lucky now. I spent the next eighteen months researching the enigmatic subject of luck. Had I known how challenging this quest would be, I might not have started. I set some tough goals for myself. They were challenging objective targets in areas that were new to me. The results hugely exceeded my expectations.

I was very lucky, and so were many of my clients. I am going to share some of their lucky secrets so that you can get lucky, too. My goal now is to help you find more luck in your life. You will be the sole judge of whether I used my time productively. I truly hope I did.

Introduction

EVERYBODY WANTS MORE luck in his or her life. Is this possible? The truth is that it is possible, and there are some very logical reasons to explain why this is so. There are also some extremely illogical reasons, and these are more difficult to explain.

While researching for this book, I became increasingly fascinated by the illogical concepts and the philosophies associated with luck. Some of these concepts have been around for centuries, whereas others are more recent.

I experimented with these techniques on myself and with my clients. I was shocked and, on occasions, frightened by some of the results. They defied logical explanation.

Could I use these techniques myself? There was only one way to find out. I chose a new project to test my techniques. It was on a subject I knew little about.

Online gambling is one of the fastest growth industries and generates billions in revenue for these companies. Some of their clients have profited, too. Others have not been so lucky.

It is now possible to bet on almost anything, including political election results and even talent TV shows. Poker is a huge market, as is sports betting. I chose predicting sports results, not least because it is a subject I follow with passion. It would still be a stiff challenge to get lucky. Did I succeed and make any money?

The answer is yes, I made money—not a huge fortune, but enough to buy a new car. Enough for three international companies to drastically limit my accounts.

How did I do this? This book will explain how, and this is a taste of what is to come.

- How do you decide exactly what you want and thereby bring life to your goals?
- How do you build confidence, even if this does not come naturally?
- How do you construct vivid visualizations that become self-fulfilling prophecies?
- How do you develop mindfulness and connect to the vast power of your unconscious mind?
- How do you use the interconnected techniques of hypnosis, HeartMath, and havening?
- Why are some people lucky, while others are not?
- How do you use synchronicity and coincidence to put luck on your side and discover that quantum physics, relativity, string theories, and the law of attraction may be related?

The overarching conclusion I reached writing this book was that luck is inextricably linked to intuition. There is much that we can do to improve our intuition. All of the secrets of success that I describe develop priceless intuition skills. Are you ready for this journey now?

Ten Months into My Get-Lucky-Now Project—November 2014

I did not have much to show for the first ten months of research, with the exception of the success of my sports-betting experiment.

It was time to start writing, so I took myself away from all the usual distractions, hoping for inspiration. This is an extract from my November 2014 blog.[1]

Get Lucky Now!

I consider myself lucky but never take this for granted. I start and finish every day reminding myself just how lucky I am now, how lucky I have been in the past, and how lucky I hope to be in the future.

I like to believe that there is an endless supply of luck available for everybody. Sadly, there is also a lot of bad luck around. If we can attract more good luck than bad luck, we are ahead of the game.

One reason that I am feeling lucky right now is that I'm in a great place. A small hotel room in a small village on the wild, untamed Portuguese Atlantic coast. It is November 2014. The weather is mild, and the surf is crashing onto a deserted beach that stretches as far as the eye can see. I am lucky to be here.

This village is thought to be lucky, too. It does not look it. Some interesting old houses, but also plenty of drab apartment blocks, some of which look abandoned. A few cafés, bars, shops, and people complete the picture. So why is this village thought to be lucky, and why do I feel especially lucky today?

The name of the village is Consolação, and many people consider it lucky. For centuries they have traveled for hundreds, even thousands, of miles to visit it. More specifically, to lie on the rocks next to the sea. They say it heals their arthritis and many other things, too.

There is also a beautiful beach, and I spent hours walking and thinking about my book. If I am writing a book about luck, my readers will expect me to be lucky, too. So how can I convince them, apart from my previous story about winning enough to buy a new car? While this was a good start, I needed more than this to show for my efforts. I didn't come up with any good ideas, and so after a few days I returned home.

I guess I was naïve and half expected to come home to some good news. So I was just a little disappointed to find that nothing had changed. No lucky breaks so far.

The next day I got lucky.

- I was awarded a lucrative voice-over contract.
- I sold my house.
- My wife received a $35,000 legacy from the estate of a man who was a total stranger.

Wow! Just in case you are wondering, these statements are all items of public record.

It suddenly occurred to me that my fascination with luck started much earlier than 2014. This thought surfaced from somewhere deep in my memory. So often light-bulb moments occur unexpectedly after periods of reflection and meditation. I recognized that my fascination with luck had been floating around in my mind for much longer. Only now were these random thoughts starting to coalesce, become more tangible, and develop a life of their own.

I Blame the Drugs

"What are those strange shapes?" I asked through my swollen and bloodied mouth.

"They are symbols of your health, wealth, and happiness," she replied with the voice of an angel.

I liked her answer a lot; it made a great deal of sense at the time. I can't remember my reply. It was probably "Far out," or "Cool," or something similar. At a deeper level, however, those three words set up a resonance that has stayed with me to this day; indeed, the resonance has continued to grow stronger each day.

It has taken me to the far corners of the world, including war-torn Angola, the swamps of Nigeria, the steppes of Kazakhstan, and the deserts of the Middle East, as I recognized that all our hopes, fears, and primeval drives are hidden deep within these four words. This is what this book is about.

Anyway, back to the drugs. While the seventies were a great time to be a student, they were not so good for wisdom teeth. I, like many others of my age, suffered from impacted wisdom teeth. *Suffered* is not an accurate description. I had no pain and was blissfully unaware of the many scary future consequences that could result if they were left untreated.

The standard treatment for this condition is extraction, and so I was sent off to the medical center. I signed the consent form, and my reluctant wisdom teeth were extracted under general anesthesia. Little did I know that while this painful procedure may have been unnecessary, it would change my life.

I recall nothing of the surgical procedure, but I do vividly remember waking up afterward. I could not move my head, my jaw felt as if it had been broken, and my vision was blurred. I was dimly aware of some strange symbols in front of my eyes.

As mentioned previously, she replied, "They are Chinese symbols on my belt buckle, and they represent luck, health, wealth, and happiness."

This book is about your luck, health, wealth, and happiness. It is also about your success and mindfulness, too. These words have clear meanings, except perhaps for mindfulness. Mindfulness is a word that is used more often now than ever before, but its meaning may not always be well understood.

One definition from Wikipedia is "bringing one's complete attention to the present experience on a moment-to-moment basis." Its supporters claim that mindfulness reduces stress, high blood pressure, anxiety, depression, and many other things.

So what does this have to do with you? Almost everything, as far as your future success is concerned. The reason is that when people are mindful and living in the present, they are capable of performing at a much higher level than they thought possible. Athletes call this "the zone"; others describe it as "being in flow."

Whatever you wish to call it, you will have likely experienced it before, and you know that it was a great feeling. At such times, it feels as if life is easy, and all you have to do is push at open doors.

How great would it be if you could have this feeling more often or even create it at will? The following chapters will point you in the right direction to achieve this state. I will use the words "luck," "health," "wealth," "happiness," "success," and "mindfulness" many times, often interchangeably. Surprisingly, success can be found in the most unlikely places, and it is a lot easier than you might think.

This book will guide you to what you really want, not what you think you might want. Health, wealth, and happiness come in many guises, but one of them will fit you perfectly.

You may be a bit skeptical and are very careful about whom you trust.

I don't blame you. I am the same. If it helps, I'll share a bit more of my background with you, along with more reasons for writing this book.

I was lucky enough to attend medical school during the seventies and even luckier to remember most of it. I was a student for five years, and the resultant lack of money was more than compensated for by the opportunities to party, play sports, learn to stitch wounds in the emergency room, and assist in operating rooms. These were my passions at the time, and so I was happy most of the time.

I also learned how to meditate. I can't remember why, but in retrospect, it was the most valuable trick I learned. My only vague memories of the meditation course I attended are that it cost money, and I didn't have much of that. I can also remember I had tickets to watch the Rolling Stones and almost missed the concert because my teacher didn't wake me up. He thought I needed the rest!

I can also remember my special mantra, about which I was sworn to secrecy. I remember thinking, "I bet everyone gets the same mantra," but for someone who should never be trusted with a secret, I have kept my promise—so far!

Since then, I have spent most of my life working in Africa as a medical doctor in challenging conditions. This included seven years in Angola during a bloody civil war and four years in Nigeria in turbulent and sometimes violent times. I was shot at, shelled, and imprisoned (briefly), and I nearly died from malaria. I took these incidents in stride but was less able to handle some of the other experiences.

As a surgeon, you are prepared to deal with serious accidents, but I was never able to feel the same way about dealing with the results of deliberate violence. I still have nightmares about it. I have seen the worst that humans can inflict on one another, but I have also seen the best. In times of hardship, the thin veneer of civilization is peeled away, and only the truth is left. More often than not, this truth reveals great strength, courage, and compassion.

Fortunately, now we have much more comfortable lives, and so it should be immeasurably easier for us to reconnect to our higher qualities—and it can be, but only if we can get out of our own way.

Time to Put on Your Party Clothes and Celebrate

Get Lucky Now! is about how to get what you want the easy way—by using mindfulness. Thousands and even millions of people have used mindfulness to achieve success throughout history. They did not have to pay millions for these secrets or even join some weird sect. They just had to discover how to use their minds more effectively.

Some lucky ones follow mindfulness unconsciously and, when asked, just describe it as "common sense." Most of us, however, have to make some effort and be prepared to look at the world in a different light.

Surprisingly, it is a lot easier than you might expect. We can all think of times in the past when doors opened effortlessly for us, as if by magic, and can remember with joy the priceless treasures that were waiting on the other side. Unfortunately, we can also remember the many other doors that remained closed, despite our best efforts to pry them open.

Of course, there is a reason for the difference. Some doors attracted you at a deep unconscious level and were just waiting for you to open them. Others repelled you, but you were so busy with your hectic life that you missed the signs. You unwittingly made your life a lot more complicated than necessary.

Life was not always like this, and it was much simpler when you were a baby. From the very first day, you were 99.99 percent ready for life. You needed parental support, but all your systems and organs were formed and functioning perfectly.

You did not need to think about your insulin metabolism or your immune system because they were automatic. They were governed by your unconscious mind. You did not really have a conscious mind at this point, but you soon began to acquire one.

Although it was only small, your conscious mind soon felt that it was the most important thing in your life and was the boss. It is not a coincidence, but this is when life also became more complicated. Is it possible to go back to the easy life, knowing what you know now? It certainly is.

Your new journey starts right now. It starts on this day and at this time. From this moment forward, you will start to learn to trust your instincts and heightened intuition and listen more attentively to your inner voice. You will delight in appreciating the critical importance of pushing at open doors and reaping the success on the other side, rather than wasting all of your time and energy pushing on the closed doors that were never meant to be opened.

The truth is that this is the secret of how to achieve success the easy way rather than the hard way. Developing mindfulness puts you in harmony with your unconscious mind; it allows you to flow, to know yourself, to let go, to see the signs, and to release more mind power than you ever believed possible.

Mindfulness works because it helps create a calm mind. A calm mind gives room to the unconscious mind to thrive and produces flow. Trust your instincts to find the open doors, and you can then enter them with confidence. Mindfulness is the foundation for building what you want for your life, not what others think you deserve.

You will start to reap the benefits from reading this book immediately. Any one chapter can propel your life to the next level. Read all the chapters, practice the exercises, and then be surprised after discovering just how high you can fly.

This book is also about magic. More specifically, it is about the magic of your mind and how you are only using a fraction of what you could be using to make your life a whole lot easier.

Magic is a special, mysterious, or inexplicable quality, talent, or skill. It is a subject that delights all children and tantalizes their imagination. Sadly, it is something that most adults reject—or do they?

Is there still some deep recess of your mind that believes that your childhood magic is still alive—a vague conviction that your universe is not quite as random as it sometimes might appear? I hope so.

A world that is limited to just laboratory results will be much smaller, less colorful, and far less happy than one overflowing with an abundance of nature's daily miracles, even if they are currently poorly understood.

So what else can you expect from this book's alchemy? Curiously, success and magic appear to be linked. While either can exist independently, their combination increases their potency many times over.

Set your sights high. The enemy of the best is the good. In other words, if you accept the good, you are far less likely to achieve the best outcome. You will delight in reconnecting with the person you were meant to be before the self-limiting beliefs exerted their restrictive influence. Soon you will be able to tune in to the creative deeper areas of your mind and see things with a new clarity.

For perhaps the first time, you will experience being the driver of your life rather than being the passenger. You are in control of your life, imposing your demands on life rather than accepting the demands that life imposes on you.

If You Can't Beat Them, Join Them

Ask yourself this question: "What do successful people do differently from me?"

In the following chapters, we will ask this question many times. We will study successful people to learn from them. Their success is not an accident. It is not just a result of luck, either. Although, intriguingly, many successful people believe that they create their own luck.

The following pages are filled with practical examples for you to use. These are based on my diverse experiences and gleaned painstakingly, and sometimes painfully, from the university of life. You can also adapt the conclusions from the great thinkers of history, because their views are as valid now as when they were living.

This book is not only about successful people but also about ordinary people like you and me. It is about people who have found success in different ways. Reassuringly, there are some common strands that have stood the test of time. At least one of these might point you in the right direction when you feel a little lost in an increasingly confusing world. Embrace two or more strands, and who knows where your journey might end?

When All Else Fails, Read the Instructions

How you use this book will determine, to a large extent, what you receive from it. It will take some commitment, but not as much as you might fear. Life would be simple if I could just let out the secrets of success now. You could then memorize them and use them immediately.

Indeed, I could share some secrets right away. I know that at least one would help you, and you would probably be very happy with it.

I'm not going to, though, for two fundamental reasons. First, you would add me to your long list of all the well-intentioned people in your life who have tried to persuade you to do stuff "for your own good." Most people's lists are way too long already.

Second, there is a much bigger prize out there almost within your reach, and certainly a lot closer than you can imagine. The secrets (that I'm not sharing just yet) are good. The ideas that come from your own mind will be so much better; indeed, they will be the best for you.

My role is only to tickle your brain. More specifically, it is to tickle the large bit of your brain that you are not using to anywhere near its full potential—your unconscious mind.

Let me give you an example. In my work as an elite performance director, it makes no difference to me whether my client is a sports star, business mogul, TV celebrity, or a friend who lives next door. When I see a client for the first time, I ask for only two things: an open mind and a brief description of the issue.

First, I want my client to have an open mind. There is no problem with skepticism; that is to be expected. Indeed, it is a healthy attitude, as long as it is combined with an open mind.

Second, I require a note detailing the issue before our session. This note is vital to me, as it describes the client's view of his or her problem at a superficial level and projects a desired outcome. Ultimately, my client will measure our success working together, or lack of it, against this yardstick.

At a deeper level, something magical often happens when my clients write their notes to me. These notes take on a life of their own. I start to appreciate the words they use, I gain a glimpse of their view of the world and what makes them tick, and I start to develop the skeletons of strategies that I believe they will find helpful.

Their notes are often anything but brief. The magic is often hidden in the final paragraph.

"Steve, I'm sorry I rambled on a bit. I hadn't thought of some of these things for years. You will be really surprised, but I feel a lot better already, just for writing this down."

We have all probably heard something similar and so are not in the least surprised, because this is how the mind works. Writing about a problem often helps. So I'd like to stress this fundamental point with you right now: writing is the doing part of thinking.

This sentence is really important, which is why it has appeared so early in this book. It is important because writing is a simple way to connect to the unconscious mind. It can put us into a flow state, like the zone in sports or the groove that musicians describe. These are creative places to be in, because these are places where many successful ideas germinate and grow.

A Color TV Will Always Be Better Than a Black-and-White One

So use this book for writing as well as reading. Scribble to your heart's content. You may use highlighters. If so, choose your colors with care. Red means "danger," right? Use your favorite color for whatever most strongly resonates with you.

I know from working with clients that some of these nuggets will help catapult you to the next level.

Use a neutral color for everything you are not sure about. In time, you will cross some of these out. Other bits will turn to your favorite color right in front of you. Whatever is left may take a long time to digest and can be safely ignored for the moment.

At the end of each chapter, you will find a "meditation booth." Briefly review the chapter, your scribbled notes, and your highlighted text. Identify three points that you believe can help you immediately (or at least in the very near future) find the open doors that surround you more easily.

Spend a few minutes thinking about how you could use these three points in some part of your life. Make a commitment to discuss these points with your friends and others you trust. These are all great ways to feed ideas into your unconscious mind so that it can digest them at its leisure.

I'll put it another way.

- Well-intentioned thoughts often remain so.
- Spoken thoughts sometimes get done.
- Written thoughts often lead to unimagined success.
- Shared thoughts propel you as high as you want to fly.

All successful coaches know that as their clients become excited by new ideas, their confidence grows and results improve. They also know that a month later, these clients are often back where they started. This is because change is difficult to cement, and it is all too easy to slip back to the comfort zone.

It is almost certain that you will find more success as a result of reading this book. Similarly, it is possible that unless you remind yourself periodically of the key insights you have discovered, you will slip back to your old thought patterns. The benefits from the work and time that you have invested will start to trickle away.

At the end of this book, I will have suggestions about how to use your "action points." Now, you are almost ready to get started. Fasten your seat belt and step on the gas.

Do you know where you are going? Can you be sure the map you are holding is accurate? Can you trust it? No, no, and no. But this is a time for courage—to go forth bravely, as somebody once said.

Dr. Sigmund Freud knew a bit about how our brains work and offered some guarded encouragement: "Illusions commend themselves to us because they save us pain and allow us to enjoy pleasure instead. We must therefore accept it without complaint when they sometimes collide with a bit of reality against which they are dashed to pieces."

For what it's worth, most people are no longer sure about what constitutes reality. "Reality is merely an illusion, albeit a very persistent one." So apparently Professor Einstein was just as unsure about reality as we are.

This complicates our mission more than a little. But at a deeper level, it also makes it a lot easier. We will frequently return to Einstein's sage words one way or another in the following chapters.

We will see what we see, or what we think we see.

Now review your notes and thoughts on this chapter.

Ask yourself this question: "What three things can I do now that can help me immediately, or at least in the very near future, to make more luck and find more health, wealth, and happiness?"

Write your three points down in the booth.

Meditation Booth
Three Nuggets for Now

1.

2.

3.

1

Goals

Do you ever feel that your life is missing something crucial, but you can't put your finger exactly on what it is? Like an irritating itch that won't go away?

You look at others enviously as they appear to achieve so much more, with apparently a lot less effort.

"What are they doing that I'm not?" You wonder why so many doors seem closed to you, and why the good things you want in your life are so elusive. Now it is time to say good-bye to this frustration and discover how to make things happen for you the easy way.

Have you ever found yourself asking these types of questions, too?

- Will Johnny gain a place at the best school in our area?
- Will Dave win the promotion he deserves so much?
- Will Debbie graduate with good grades?
- How successful will my favorite sports team or player be this season?
- How long will it take me to become pregnant?
- How can I meet my increased sales target this year?

Most of these questions will probably be very familiar to you, because they are our modern preoccupations, or even obsessions. No matter how often you ask yourself these questions, it will not change the answers.

Worse, just asking these questions will add to your frustration. These questions will drain away your precious energy and your thoughts that could be used far more productively elsewhere in your life.

It is now time for me to reveal the first secret of getting lucky. It is also time for you to stop asking these questions, lose your frustration, and discover how to make things happen for you the easy way. From now on, just push at the open doors. I will explain what I mean by this in a moment. But first, let me shake your foundations a little.

From an early age, you will have been told that the harder you work, the more successful you will be. The sooner you can throw away this well-intentioned but mistaken advice, the sooner you will start to live the life you deserve.

There are countless examples to demonstrate that the more you strive for success, the more elusive it becomes. You will probably remember times in your life when you just wanted something so badly that you could barely think about anything else.

Much more important is taking one moment at a time to stay in the present. The result is peak performance, also known as being in "the zone" or "flow." This is what this book is about—how to attract more of what you want, with a lot less stress; not to be dragged back by the past or worry about the future; and to just stay in the present so that you recognize the opportunities that surround you.

You might expect that the world of business would have found the keys to unlocking peak performance in employees and managers. Sadly, many companies have no clue. Indeed, not for the first time in history, they have it completely wrong.

Would the banking crisis have happened if employees had been encouraged to do the best job they could each day rather than devising complex future strategies that took them further away from what their customers wanted? Perhaps not, but at least their managers might have heard the warning bells earlier.

The banks are just one of many examples. This obsession with results infects schools, hospitals, corporations, sports teams, and many other organizations. It infects each of us to varying degrees, too.

How often have you heard people say, "If you can't measure it, you can't manage it?" I spent many years reciting this mantra. Worse, I even believed it, but now I understand its limitations. I hope I can persuade you of its limitations, too.

Unfortunately, society is far less concerned with the more important subject of our day-to-day activities. This is a disastrous error, because how we choose to spend each minute of each day is one of the few things in life that we can control. Such moments form the building blocks that can shape our futures and our successes. Valuing these moments allows us to "stay in the present."

The truth is that the more you measure things—especially results—the more elusive they become. I am not for a moment saying that results are not important. They are, but not when considered in isolation. Far more important are the small steps you take every day that produce these results.

Small steps are the foundation of the Japanese business model known as *kaizen*. Take these little steps in the right direction and at the right time, and your eventual success is guaranteed. Just push at the open doors as they manifest, and ignore the closed ones. Leave them for others who might them more suitable.

Self-Knowledge

Happy people know who they are, what they want, and how to achieve their goals. That is why they are lucky. You have started on your journey to attract more luck, too.

The mysterious doors of life surround you, and their importance to you is beyond measure. Everything you want and everything you will ever want lies behind these doors—just tantalizingly out of reach.

Some doors call out to you to approach them for all the wrong reasons, whereas others beg you to draw near for all the right reasons. Some just scream for you to go away. Usually, you would be right to give these doors a wide berth, but not always. This is rather confusing. Which doors should you push at to enter, and where is the best place for you to start?

When you were a child bursting to share a story or a magical moment, your words tumbled out in no particular order, leaving you very frustrated. The listener probably looked at you with a wry smile. Your wise friend, teacher, or parent implored, "Take your time, take a deep breath, and start from the beginning."

This is good advice for anybody, anywhere, and always has been.

Our friend Aristotle also knew a thing or two about what makes us tick. He explained a long time ago: "Knowing yourself is the beginning of all wisdom."

Successful people know which doors are the easiest to open, but probably take for granted their ability to identify these as normal. They are also probably bemused by how difficult we make our lives, because we continue to go in circles around doors that remain resolutely closed.

The truth is that most of us struggle with developing and sustaining a sense of purpose; many of our ancestors did, too. This is why this chapter is so important and is the logical starting point of our journey.

Not much has changed over the last three thousand years. When the same message of the importance of self-knowledge keeps surfacing repeatedly over the centuries, we can be fairly sure of its enduring value.

More recently, Nietzsche described the difficulty attached to truly resonating with one's own unique personality. He would have known this more intimately than most people. Nietzsche died in 1900, eleven years after suffering a serious nervous breakdown. We can only wonder and hope that his eventual self-realization provided comfort during his final years.

"One's own self is well hidden from one's own self; of all mines of treasure, one's own is the last to be dug up."

Let us ensure your treasure surfaces much sooner. You have a busy life, many challenges, and many people competing for a piece of your time. When you have chosen to live in the "now," you do not have the luxury to explore all the doors around you. You want what you desire, and you want it right away.

This will be difficult, if not impossible, without such self-knowledge. This is your shortcut and the way to connect to your intuitive self—to do what feels right, to get out of your own way, and to allow yourself to be guided to the doors meant for you.

Possessing accurate self-knowledge is critical in building a healthy, wealthy, and happy life. Although for some, it is about the hardest thing in life to achieve, for others it is as natural as walking down the stairs. Fortunately, you do not need to spend years in contemplation and meditation searching for perfection. Like so many other things in life, you just need to be a bit more skillful than you might be at present. A little goes a very long way.

The reason self-knowledge is so important is that with it we can plan our lives and develop authentic goals to structure order from chaos by pushing at the open doors and undercutting our own luck. Without self-knowledge we drift, or even worse, we waste our time and energy on goals that are meaningless or beyond our control. These are the closed doors and were always meant to be—at least for you.

How to Choose a Wonderful Goal

Goals are, therefore, critical. If you do not know where you are going, then any road will take you there; it will be a long journey, and it may not be a happy one. The shortest route lies in choosing the correct goal.

Ideally, you should have one overarching goal in life. I suggest that you take some time before deciding what this might be. It is very easy to think of an impressive goal. But is it the correct one? Is it something you want to achieve, or something that your parents, teachers, or friends have recommended? Is it a goal that society regards as worthy, rather than something you have always wanted to do?

Motivational guru Tony Robbins gives a stark and somewhat nihilistic message of the dangers that haunt the unwary: "You will become by and large what your friends expect you to become."

This might feel like the easier path—to conform to others' expectations of you. But we know on the inside when something is missing. In time, this feeling builds dissatisfaction and even stress. Nothing clouds your judgment and performance more certainly than stress, especially if it is prolonged.

As mentioned previously, you can only develop your goals with confidence when you have a deep understanding of yourself, your values, and your beliefs. This book will provide helpful tips to nudge you a little further along your path of self-awareness.

Perhaps you, like many people, are not sure what your wonderful goal might be. When people follow their passion, they are rarely disappointed. How do you spend your money at present, after having paid all the bills? If your credit-card statement reveals more bills for surfboards and accessories than anything else, then does this perhaps suggest a career in surfing or another sport?

How do you spend your free time? What activity makes time fly, fills you with deep contentment either during or after, and, in a humble and grounded way, lets you know that this is something you are rather good at?

If you are still struggling to identify what makes you happy and how are you would like to spend the rest of your life, you might like to try this simple exercise.

I hope that you are happy and healthy right now. I normally encourage only positive thoughts, but there is always an exception to every rule. This is it.

Spend just a few moments imagining how you would feel if you had just been told that you only had six more months to live. How would you use this time? What would you do differently? What would each day look and feel like?

Now readjust yourself to your present situation. Are any of the changes you considered just a few moments ago still appropriate? If so, what would it take to make them possible? Is it possible that from your reflection you can find the inspiration that Churchill describes? "We shall draw from the heart of suffering itself the means of inspiration and survival."

I hope you now have an outline picture in your mind about what you wish to achieve. Mark Twain understood the importance of self-knowledge and often observed lack of clarity among his circle of acquaintances when he said, "I can teach anybody how to get what they want out of life. The problem is that I can't find anybody who can tell me what they want."

After you have read this book, you will have a clearer picture of what you want, more ideas on how to achieve it, and the tools to make it easier than you dreamed.

You will also have a clearer idea of what you really want, a lot more ideas about how to achieve your goals, and the tools to make it so much easier than you dreamed.

You lucky person!

Bring Life to Your Goal

For most of your life at school, at work, and at home, you have been conditioned, to a certain extent, to recognize success by the monetary value of your possessions. Society places less value on qualities that cannot be so easily measured and yet are far more important.

There is nothing wrong with material goals. In this affluent world, most of us dream of big houses, big cars, and fat bank balances but forget those who cannot even dream of their next meal.

So make your goal a means to an end and the result of doing other things skillfully along the way. When you reach your goal, do not be surprised when you look back and realize that the real fun was the journey, not the destination.

In his book *Awaken the Giant Within*, Tony Robbins makes another powerful point that is well worth more careful thought: "Achieving goals by themselves will never make us happy in the long term; it's who you become, as you overcome the obstacles necessary to achieve your goals, that can give you the deepest and most long-lasting sense of fulfillment."

Many mountaineers describe a sensation of anticlimax after a particularly difficult climb. They remember with much more lasting satisfaction the journey that took them there. Athletes who have trained for years to win an Olympic gold medal enjoy a temporary euphoria that is often replaced by a vague sadness or even depression. Their goal was their life. So what is left when their goal has been achieved?

Certainly dream of that big house and enjoy it when you own it; however, do not be surprised that once you own your new house, your goal has changed its shape, to a greater or lesser extent.

If it was for an even bigger house, then there may be many more house moves in store for you. If it is a new goal that germinated during the journey, then perhaps you stumbled across some unexpected open doors. This is what people call "serendipity," "coincidence," "synchronicity," or just "a healthy dose of luck." We will talk much more about this in later chapters.

Let us return to the present. Once you have decided on your goal, the more different ways you can remind yourself of it each day, the more successful you are likely to be. There are many ways to do this. Examples include writing the goal on sticky notes and sticking them on the bathroom mirror and the refrigerator or using the goal as the screensaver on your computer, mobile phone, and alarm clock.

The more places you can think of to display your notes, the more likely you are to reach your goal. It directs your unconscious mind and helps build a self-fulfilling prophecy. Keep in mind that writing is the doing part of thinking. It is a powerful connection to your unconscious mind. President Lincoln had no doubt about the importance of personal goals. As Lincoln said, "A goal properly set is halfway reached."

Olympic swimming champion Michael Phelps is a great example of the importance of constant reminders. When he announced his goal of eight gold medals in the China Olympics, he was incensed reading an article expressing doubts about his ability to deliver this prediction. He pinned this article to his locker and stared at it every morning until he left for China. Was this visualization? Was it a powerful affirmation? Was it a self-fulfilling prophecy? Who knows? But the important thing is that it worked for him.

Phelps said, "People say that I have great talent, but in my opinion excellence has nothing to do with talent. It is about what you choose to believe and how determined you are to get there. The mind is more powerful than anything else."[2]

It certainly is. So each chapter will provide opportunities for you to explore your own mind in new ways; to open doors to your mind that you never knew existed; and to open doors to more luck, health, wealth, and happiness than you thought possible.

The Ultimate Goal Is Not to Have One

At the risk of further muddying the murky waters, let me tell you what you might have already guessed: the ultimate goal is to have no goal at all. When one's mind, body, and soul are seamlessly linked in the appreciation of the moment, then other goals are just not necessary. Magical results surface, as if from nowhere.

Very few people achieve this degree of detachment; the rest of us must continue to rely upon our goals. These are the goals that we have constructed with as much care and insight as we can. They will be more than sufficient to enrich our lives and provide much inspiration during the journey.

Do not worry if your goal is still unclear, or indeed if it should change while reading this book—or later. You'll see further information on how to get started on this in the conclusion, and then you will be more than ready to join the lucky people.

Often, all that is necessary is to be more in touch with our world—moment by moment. This will be the constant strand throughout this book.

Author Robert Pirsig has provided me with much inspiration since my student days. I have read *Zen and the Art of Motorcycle Maintenance* countless times. Although his messages are not the easiest to decipher, I think I know (but easily could be wrong) what he means when he says, "It is a puzzling thing. The truth knocks on the door and you say, 'Go away, I'm looking for the truth,' and so it goes away. Puzzling."

How many truths do we not see because our minds are elsewhere? How much of our precious time have we wasted searching for something that cannot be found but can only be perceived through intuition?

We have enjoyed enough puzzles for the moment.

Our brains love questions, and the response is always more creative than when we just follow orders.

Now review your notes and thoughts on this chapter.

Ask yourself this question: "What three things can I do now that can help me immediately, or at least in the very near future, to make more luck and find more health, wealth, and happiness?"

Write your three points down in the booth.

In the next chapter, we will continue our journey and examine the importance of self-esteem to our success. We will discover how the power of our thoughts can create a massive and positive effect on our confidence.

Meditation Booth
Three Nuggets for Now

1.

2.

3.

2

Confidence

CONFIDENCE IS A very influential component for getting lucky, and it is therefore the second secret. It should come as no surprise that lucky people have a great amount of confidence. The rest of us look enviously at them and wish that we could be more confident, too. The truth is that you can be. Here are several simple techniques that you can practice to attract more confidence into your life. You will then also invite a lot more luck.

People often make unselfish and courageous decisions to help others, sometimes by even risking their lives. When asked to justify their actions, common responses are, "Because I have to look at myself in the bathroom mirror every morning," or "I just did what anybody in the same situation would have done."

You also have to look at yourself every day, and what you see in the mirror will dictate what you feel about yourself, good or bad. It will determine how confident you feel. It may be your physical appearance or your assessment of your personality or what you have achieved in your life.

For many people, their assessments of themselves will be highly critical. They do not think they are good enough to hit their targets. They think not of the success they can achieve but of the barriers to overcome to get there. Their thoughts spiral into a circle of negativity, until finally they convince themselves that their project is beyond them, and they give up—often much closer to the success they deserve than they realize.

William Shakespeare used fewer words in his play *Measure for Measure* but with an even more powerful message. At times of doubt, recall his words and redouble your efforts: "Our doubts are traitors, and make us lose the good we oft might win, by fearing to attempt."

Unfortunately, harsh self-criticism destroys confidence, which further reinforces this cycle of negativity. This will not help your search for success. It will not help you find the intuitive mind-set that will identify open doors. So how can you break this destructive cycle? Fortunately, it may be far easier than you think.

Internal Dialogue

This is the voice in your brain. There is often a constant broadcast of your life. Very often, it slips out of the mouth, usually followed by an embarrassed, "I was just talking to myself."

Confidence is a state of mind and, therefore, to a greater or lesser extent, under your control. Your thoughts control your mood, and very often what goes on in your head comes out in your life. Henry Ford expressed this succinctly when he said, "Whether you think you can or think you can't—you are right."

If you think something bad will happen, chances are you will not be surprised when it does. Fortunately, the opposite is also true. Develop a positive attitude, value your talents, and approach challenges in this light, and your chances of success will increase significantly, further strengthening your confidence for future challenges.

This is the first tip that will demonstrate how you can build more confidence. Adopt this simple mantra right now. Say it out loud.

"From this moment forward, I will only say good things about myself."

If you are concerned that you might lose out on learning from your mistakes or that you are becoming arrogant, you can add the following words: "Fear not. I can trust family, friends, and the rest of the world to point out my mistakes. I do not need to give them any help."

Remember the Good Times

There are other ways to increase your confidence and self-esteem. As with most things in life, it will require some preparation and effort on your part. However, when compared with the size of the glittering prize out there, it will be one of the best investments you have ever made.

A powerful starting point is to make this commitment. Write it down; you are much more likely to keep to it. Say it aloud, too, with conviction.

"From this moment forward, I will remember every good thing that happens to me."

Unfortunately, most people have a brilliant memory of all the things that have gone wrong in their lives but struggle to think of the many things that went right.

So when somebody says something complimentary to you, revel in the simple pleasure for a second or two longer than you ordinarily would before allowing that memory to slip into your unconscious mind. If you can do this several times a day for a month, there will be a subtle change in your brain chemistry and outlook on life. You will notice the difference. Those closest to you will notice it more.

You can enhance this effect by subtly giving your brain another push in the right direction. When you have one of these pleasurable experiences, make sure that the memory is easier to retrieve by associating it with a physical anchor. This is the memory equivalent of underlining or highlighting a statement in an article.

Some people press their thumb and forefinger together to reinforce a happy memory. Others touch their ear or brush their pants. Spend some time choosing your anchor. It should be discreet, but, most important, it should feel right.

Adopt this practice for a month, and chances are that you will continue in the future. These anchors will become seamless and automatic parts of your life.

Once you have mastered this technique, you will be ready for an advanced anchoring technique. This can be very powerful, but it requires you to be in a relaxed mental state for the best results.

Think of when you were deeply experiencing flow. Whatever it was that you were doing, it felt very easy, natural, and relaxed. At that time, you felt that you could do no wrong. You probably wished that you could bottle that special feeling so that you could take it away and then reproduce it in the future whenever you needed it most.

The following technique does not require a bottle, but it can help you to enter your flow state a lot easier and quicker than you ordinarily would.

Take your thoughts back to this special occasion and use your memory to add some detail to the picture of this event in your mind. Where were you? What was the date? Who were you with? What clothes were you wearing? Do you remember any of the conversations with others? What other details can you add to this event?

When you are ready, take your time and answer this special question: In only one word, how would you describe your feeling on this special day?

Then answer this next question: If the special word had a color, what would it be?

Now we come to the most important question: How can you use this word and color to remind yourself of this special day when you were experiencing flow, so that when you need to reproduce the same mental state in the future, you will be able to do so just as easily?

Look Like You Feel and Feel Like You Look

There are many other powerful tools to enrich confidence. Here is another example. Think for a moment of a person who is nervous, or how you might look and feel when worried.

A nervous person trembles, adopts a withdrawn posture, and keeps the head held down. The eyes shift quickly, as does the rest of the body. This arousal is due to the physiological changes associated with the overstimulation of the autonomic sympathetic nervous system and the resultant effects of adrenaline and other hormones.

This is known as the fight-or-flight response. If we hooked this person up to a biological monitor, we would record many other physiological changes, including an increased heart rate, increased breathing rate, increased blood pressure, sweaty palms, and dry mouth.

These changes prepare the body for instant action and, in the short term, are therefore valuable. In our modern society, however, much of our stress is due to emotional factors rather than causes that require immediate physical effort. The result is that we do not burn off the adrenaline and other hormones and so live in a constant state of stress and arousal. The medical consequences may be dire and include higher risks of hypertension, heart problems, anxiety, depression, and even cancer.

The personal consequences are equally serious. You will find it difficult, if not impossible, to connect to your unconscious mind. You will not find the open doors and may even be drawn to the doors that are best left alone.

Stress is a killer. It takes life, it spoils life, and it gets in the way of attracting luck into your life. The good news is that there are several ways to eliminate stress or at least control it.

The autonomic nervous system was thought to be beyond our conscious control. Now there is clear evidence that a degree of control is possible. This provides opportunities to overcome some of the dangerous effects of stress. For example, Olympic archers and pistol and rifle athletes have learned how to control their heart rate to maintain a steady aim. Perhaps snooker and darts players have, too, as have many top golfers. In later chapters, we will examine some of the methods they might use.

One simple technique you can execute right now is to adopt a confident posture. This is the opposite of the previous nervous posture. Stand or sit tall, breathe deeply and slowly, move calmly, and smile.

Smiling is particularly important. If you don't believe me, put a pencil between your teeth. This stretches the same muscles that are used when smiling, and so the pencil between your lips will make you feel a little bit happier.

These are examples of how the mind can affect our physiology, and the opposite is equally true. The mind and body are seamlessly linked, and by using these techniques, we can learn to use these to our advantage.

Milton Erickson, the father of American medical hypnosis, also fully appreciated the effect of posture on confidence. He would instruct his chronically depressed patients to walk home rather than use public transport and count the chimneys on the way.

One reason for his curious directive is that doing something, especially if depressed, is always better than doing nothing. There is also no way to avoid looking up and adopting a tall posture when counting chimneys. Not surprisingly, his patients reported feeling somewhat better, but they were not sure why!

This book will explore mental strategies to overcome and eventually master these natural physiological responses in more detail throughout. Such strategies include the role of breathing, meditation, mindfulness, hypnosis, visualization, and other ways to "stay in the present."

Our brains love questions, and the response is always more creative than when we just follow orders. Now review your notes and thoughts on this chapter.

Ask yourself this question: "What three things can I do now that can help me immediately, or at least in the very near future, to make more luck and find more health, wealth, and happiness?"

Write your three points down in the booth. In the next chapter, we will continue our journey and examine the importance of visualization to our success. We will discover how the power of our thoughts can create a self-fulfilling prophecy of success.

Meditation Booth
Three Nuggets for Now

1.

2.

3.

3

Visualization

LUCKY PEOPLE AND successful people share one very important characteristic: they have a very clear picture in their head of what they want to achieve. This is sometimes known as visualization. This is the third of the seven secrets of getting lucky.

A vivid picture is a descriptive shortcut that takes fewer nerve cells to process than a verbal narrative. Hence the expression, "a picture is worth a thousand words."

This picture is both a goal and a focus of concentration. Very often, what you see is what you get, so make sure that it is something that you really want and not something that you are trying to avoid. The brain often does not hear *no* or *not*, sometimes with terrible results.

The world of sport is full of examples—a sprinter focusing on not starting before the gun is fired, a basketball player focusing on not missing this penalty, a golfer focusing on not driving his ball into the lake, etc. Guess what happens next? Focusing on what you want rather than what you do not want to happen is equally important in your business and personal life.

Some people are naturally very good at visualizing exactly what their body or mind is doing and what they want it to do. The good news is that these visualization skills can be taught and are available for everybody.

Most, if not all, great athletes have incredible visualization skills. Their imaginations are so creative that they may be a little embarrassed about describing their visualizations to others.

Muhammad Ali, perhaps the greatest boxer of all time, developed powerful visualization skills. One of my colleagues met him and asked the secret of his success. He sighed wearily and explained again for the thousandth time, "I float like a butterfly and sting like a bee."

My friend understood the "sting," but he was still confused by the "butterfly" metaphor. Muhammad Ali leaned closer and whispered, "I imagine floating out of my body like a butterfly."

He imagined that he was standing at each corner of the ring and watching the fight from above. When he saw a muscle ripple in the shoulder of his opponent, he knew what type of punch was coming his way and had more time to avoid it.

Great scientists also have highly developed visualization skills, especially those who work with abstract concepts. Albert Einstein is a famous example and had magical visualizations, too. He explained that most of his creative thoughts were in pictures and that he rarely thought in words. This is another proof that a picture, or visualization, is worth more than a thousand words.

These days, athletes are spending more time daydreaming with their eyes closed and less time in the gym or on the sports pitch. They are not lazy, nor are they wasting their time. What they are indulging in is deep mental practice.

The following example describes how competition skiers prepare for a downhill run. Physiologists wire their muscles and attach them to recording machines, and this science is called electromyography. They have discovered that when skiers stand in the laboratory with their eyes closed and visualize their next competition run, the same muscle groups are flexed at the same time as would happen on the real run, mirroring the ski terrain.

This is called "covert practice," as described by Dr. Simon Jenkins, principal lecturer in sports coaching. "Covert (rather than overt) practice of a skill in that no actual movement occurs. It involves the use of imagery and verbal thoughts."

Jenkins confirms the value of mental practice, too, from a scientific standpoint. "There is evidence to suggest that mental practice is better than no practice, and that mental practice in combination with physical practice is even better."

If you are still not convinced, then this famous example may be the clincher. It was written by Hirini Reedy.[3] It is also quoted by Mihaly Csikszentmihalyi in his legendary book, *Flow*.

Major James Nesbeth spent seven years as a prisoner of war in North Vietnam. During those seven years, he was imprisoned in a cage that was approximately four and one-half feet high and five long. During almost the entire time he was imprisoned he saw no one, talked to no one and experienced no physical activity. In order to keep his sanity and his mind active, he used the art of visualisation.

Every day in his mind, he would play a game of golf. A full 18-hole game at his favourite course. In his mind, he would create the trees, the smell of the freshly trimmed grass, the wind, the songs of the birds. He created different weather conditions—windy spring days, overcast winter days and sunny summer mornings. He felt the grip of the club in his hands as he played his shots in his mind. The set-up, the down-swing and the follow-through on each shot. Watched the ball arc down the fairway and land at the exact spot he had selected. All in his mind.

He did this seven days a week. Four hours a day. Eighteen holes. Seven years. When Major Nesbeth was finally released, he found that he had cut 20 strokes off his golfing average without having touched a golf club in seven years.

So now you are ready to develop your own visualization of success and join the lucky people. Fortunately, you will not have to pay for an air ticket to Vietnam to learn these skills.

Make Sense of Your Five Senses and Go Large with Your Movie

Great movie directors know the importance of creating vivid imagery using all our senses. We have five senses—sight, hearing, touch, taste, and smell. These senses are our only information channels from our environment—an environment that is limitless in its abundant diversity. Everything is channeled through these conduits.

Now it is time for you to direct your own movie. Make sure it is packed with detail relating to your five senses.

So let us get the cameras rolling. Lie back, close your eyes, and imagine some success you desire in the future, perhaps a few months away. Imagine something that you really want.

Picture yourself achieving this success in as much detail as possible, using all your five senses. Then reflect on all the things that went right over the preceding months to position you for this success. You recognize that your processes were sound and that your journey was a series of small steps. Not all of them seemed to be in the correct direction at the time.

Your thoughts are interrupted as a journalist from the local paper approaches you and asks you for the secret of your amazing success. Could you pass on some tips that would interest and help the readers of her paper?

Pause for thought for a few seconds. Then share some of the most illuminating insights and suggestions that you found the most useful in achieving this wonderful result.

Most people like being asked to help others, and this is one of the reasons why this simple visualization can be so powerful. What you have also done is change your perspective. You have permitted your mind to create a vivid movie of a positive outcome in the future. You have also changed your perspective by being the observer and watching yourself behave with unconscious excellence in this movie.

Whenever you consciously change your perspective, you always profit from this new viewpoint. Besides, you will see yourself with greater clarity and more like how others see you.

Sometimes, there is a danger that future goals can feel very remote and may even discourage you from starting your journey. When projects are broken down into small steps, however, the most impossible task suddenly seems much more reachable.

The following final visualization brings together many of the concepts that I have already described.

You have spent time choosing your goals wisely. You know all the skills that will be necessary to reach your goal. You have practiced your confidence techniques, but you are still not certain that your ability is equal to the task. This negative thought decreases your chance of being successful.

So guide your mind in a different direction and ask yourself this question: "Whom do I know who has all the skills I will need?" You do not need to know this person directly. It could be a famous celebrity, scientist, or sports personality.

Close your eyes and imagine that you are being introduced to this person. He or she is happy to talk to you, and you have all the time in the world to ask your questions and listen to his or her advice. Now stretch your creativity even further and imagine that you are floating into this other person's body and seeing the world through his or her eyes and feeling through his or her senses.

This exercise will help you to gain an understanding of the skills you need and the confidence to use them. We greatly underestimate our own abilities, and often all that is necessary to release them is to change our perspective.

So now you are ready to develop even more of your own visualizations in different areas of your life and join the lucky people. You'll see further information on how to get started on this in the conclusion.

This is sufficient for now and is a natural point to end this chapter. Now review your notes and thoughts on this chapter.

Ask yourself this question: "What three things can I do now that can help me immediately, or at least in the very near future, to make more luck and find more health, wealth, and happiness?"

Write your three points down in the booth.

In the next chapter, we will continue our journey and examine the critical importance of mindfulness and how it can also help us to get lucky.

Meditation Booth
Three Nuggets for Now

1.

2.

3.

4

Mindfulness

MINDFULNESS IS GAINING increasing popularity as a mind-control technique. It is being taught to patients in hospitals, children in schools, and business executives as part of their management development. Mindfulness has helped so many people get lucky that it is deservedly secret number four.

It is a word that is relatively easy to define, but it is far more difficult to explain why mindfulness can be of so much benefit and how it should be used.

Few would argue about this Apple Pages dictionary definition: "A mental state achieved by focusing one's awareness on the present moment, while calmly acknowledging and accepting one's feelings, thoughts, and bodily sensations, used as a therapeutic technique."

The last few words—"used as a therapeutic technique"—poses a number of important questions, particularly, "How can I use this technique on myself to develop mindfulness?"

The Tip of the Iceberg

Before I attempt to answer this question, it will be helpful to discover just a little more about how our brains work, especially with regard to our emotions.

The truth is that the brain remains one of the last barriers to scientists. Neurophysiologists have barely begun to unravel the secrets. What we do know is that we use but a fraction of the brain's potential. There are some parts of our brains that are rusty or that we have forgotten how to use. As with any part of the body and mind, we must use it or lose it. This includes the control of our emotions.

So what are emotions? Emotions and gut feelings are possibly shortcuts that the brain uses to process huge amounts of information and chunk them down to a more manageable size.

The advantage is that this will speed up your thoughts and decisions. The disadvantage is that very often you will not understand why you acted in a certain way. You might even have experienced the same situation the previous day and acted in a completely different way.

This can be very confusing. If you cannot understand how you reached a decision, what hope is there to understand the actions of others?

As self-development writer and lecturer Dale Carnegie reasoned, it is important to recognize that "when dealing with people, remember you are not dealing with creatures of logic, but creatures of emotion."

How you feel at any given moment depends on chemical changes in the brain. Through the ages, many have discovered the mind-altering properties of alcohol, cannabis, LSD, and legions of other external chemicals.

Fewer have discovered the much more valuable and helpful secret that the body, especially the brain, makes its own chemicals, which control your emotions. These chemicals include neurotransmitters such as serotonin, dopamine, and noradrenaline. Usually manufactured with perfect purity, these chemicals interact with one another in exquisite balance. This is just one of the many miracles in your body that is working in the background every moment of every day, and you are totally unaware of it.

The science behind these chemical interactions is staggeringly complex. Brilliant scientists have already developed drugs to treat conditions such as anxiety, depression, attention-deficit disorders, Parkinson's disease, and schizophrenia. As more and more discoveries are made each year, without a doubt, more Nobel prizes will be awarded, too.

These drugs can be of enormous benefit to patients, especially those with the more serious afflictions. The potential danger of any drug, however, is that it can reinforce the belief that there is a pill for every ill. This leads us adopt a passive approach to our emotions and state of mind and makes us forget that we can exert a degree of control over the neurotransmitters.

Adopting an active approach will not result in positive changes overnight. A month seems to be about the minimum time required to cement a permanent change in behavior, which means that is the minimum time you will need to commit to. By then, any benefits should be clear, and you will not want to go back to your previous situation.

House of Cards

If I thought it was easy to develop mindfulness, I would say so. It is not. Before I even attempt to provide a solution for your consideration, I will add more detail to the challenge facing us.

Our minds are normally in a state of utter chaos. No wonder the quality of our decisions is often a lot less than we would wish for. Our thoughts are riddled with doubt, guilt, and uncertainty. We often hear ourselves, and others, complain that we are of two minds about the right thing to do. If only! There are often many more options competing for our attention.

Ignorance is not a lack of the ability to see the world as it is but a disregard of what our senses and thoughts are telling us. The reality is that we have millions of different thoughts competing for our attention at any one time. It is as if there is a council in session inside our heads.

Its members represent every possible shade of political opinion, and the member who shouts the loudest usually gets heard. This helps to explain why we can reach two or more completely different decisions on the same subject within hours, or even seconds.

It also goes some way toward explaining the complex conundrum of why a single person or nation can be capable of both the most generous acts of kindness to strangers and the perpetration of the most brutal depravities on others.

The ultimate goal of developing mindfulness is a quiet mind. Inside this tranquil head, the council converses softly, the members examine and debate an issue from every angle and take turns to speak, the others listen intently, consensus builds up slowly, and the wisest member speaks last.

The German philosopher Hans Margolius would doubtless agree. He wrote, "Only in quiet waters do things mirror themselves undistorted. Only in a quiet mind is there adequate perception of the world."

So worldly perception is the prize that is almost within our grasp. Now we can begin to develop strategies that will help us become more mindful. This next bit is very important, but it took me a long time to work it out.

Back to Nature

There is nothing that you can do to develop mindfulness. Mindfulness is your natural state and has existed from the time of your birth, if not before. The problem is that you have changed from your natural state to an emotional state. For the best possible reasons, you have allowed your conscious mind far too much control. You are thinking of too many unnecessary or far less important things. If you want great examples of mindfulness, then study your pets. Your dogs, cats, horses, parakeets, and even goldfish are probably more mindful than you, because they live in the now.

I have lived for much of my life in Africa. Like many doctors before me, I soon became aware of the relative rarity of neurotic illness in the local population compared with Westerners. There are probably several reasons for this difference, but one of them might be that people living in poverty in a war zone with poor medical care just do not have time to worry about the past or the future. All of their concentration and focus must rest on what is happening at this moment and staying alive.

My clients, on the other, are either running away from an uncomfortable past or running toward a more desirable future. Often they are doing both. As a therapist, I know that I can't alter their past, but I can change the way my clients view it. We all carry some baggage from the past that slows us down, so we have to lighten this load before we can skip happily in the direction of a better future.

So developing mindfulness is a contradiction. You do not require any new tools, because you already have them. Instead, your challenge is to return to the human being that you were before other people or experiences complicated your life.

As a therapist, I am going to offer some unusual advice: stop doing things rather than start doing new things. The rest of this chapter will provide you with more suggestions.

So what are the distractions most likely to destroy mindfulness?

Can't Live with Them, Can't Live without Them

Our brains are like computers. We can only handle so much information at any one time. When our brains are overloaded, they slow down or even freeze—much like the Windows blue screen of death.

Computers work fastest and are most reliable when only one program is running, because there is less chance of software incompatibility. Of course our brains are vastly more powerful than computers and will continue to be so for the foreseeable future, but they still have their limits. They, too, work best when only a few programs are open.

A conscientious computer owner runs only programs that are being worked on and defragments the hard disk regularly to free up space and increase processing power.

Few people take the same care with their brain. They lose themselves in the background noise. Overloading your brain puts you at the risk of not being able to find some of your most precious gifts.

Hans Hofmann was one of those rare individuals who could combine the rigorous disciplines of science and mathematics with abstract expressionist art and still find time to think. Perhaps his secret to success was an exceptionally ordered mind. His approach was one of ruthless simplification: "The ability to simplify means to eliminate the unnecessary so that the necessary may speak."

In other words, allow room for the unconscious mind to speak. While it might appear to us that our brains are unlimited in their power, there are limits. While it is true that they possess enormous memory and can handle huge amounts of data, there are nevertheless some boundaries. Scientists have established that our brains can only handle seven packets of information at any one time.

Once this limit is exceeded, the pure information is corrupted. While the content remains identical at a deep level, the overlying abbreviated information could be quite different. This is one reason why sometimes we have so much difficulty communicating with each other.

These information shortcuts have evolutionary importance and can, on occasion, be directly linked to our survival. That is why we still have them. When Mr. Caveman is confronted with a saber-toothed tiger, he does not have time to consider all the details of his situation. Fight or flight—that is the only decision he has time to make, and he needs to make it right now.

If he were to think of too many options at the same time, he would freeze, paralyzed by fear. This would be the worst possible outcome. We have all frozen at some time, and it is not a pleasant feeling. It is not as bad as being eaten by a tiger, though.

Why Don't You Listen to What I Say?

The most common shortcuts our brains use to condense information are generalization, deletion, and distortion. Conversation would be rather boring without these shortcuts. In other words, we do not need to discuss every detail of our thoughts. Much can be omitted. What is left is colored by whatever emotional lens we happen to be wearing that day—whether they're rose-tinted glasses or something darker.

As we drone on about our terrible day at the office and the other person receives this information, the same processes apply. When our story is recounted to yet another person, who again uses the same processes, there may not be much of the original story left. This is one of the reasons why people get things wrong, why couples divorce, and why countries go to war.

Thus, if our success depends on the quality of our thoughts, and our thoughts depend on the power of our brain, then we can take some very obvious steps to increase our chances of success. The simplest step is to limit the amount of information we allow in.

Chinese writer Lin Yutang was another gifted individual who was also able to combine his literary talents with those of an accomplished inventor. Sometimes what we don't do is more important than what we do. His conclusion was very similar to Hofmann's ruthless elimination of the unnecessary, as mentioned previously: "Besides the noble art of getting things done, there is the noble art of leaving things undone. The wisdom of life consists in the elimination of non-essentials."

We all love to feel as if we are busy and usually choose the easiest and, hence, the least important task to address first. Far harder is to stop, do nothing, and just think. This is unfortunate, because when we are in this optimum state of mindfulness, we are ready for the next step, which is to process incoming information with maximum efficiency.

The processing choices are simple, as there are only three. We can act on information, file it away, or delete it. Another word for this is concentration.

Contrary to what we might say to others, we do not lose our concentration. At any one time, there are just too many places for it to go to. It is not lost; it has just gone somewhere else.

The truth is that people are happiest when they are totally absorbed in just one task. Time flies, the ego is for once subservient, and we become almost totally unaware of our environment. Without consciously recognizing it, we unconsciously enter a magical self-hypnotic state.

Our normal state of mind is chaotic and does not feel so comfortable. This chaos should not come as a surprise. We are now surrounded by so much up-to-the-second information, which bombards us from the TV, radio, newspapers, social-network contacts, breaking news, text messages, telephones, diary reminders, and e-mails. So if you want to find the optimum state of mindfulness, how can you limit the information you allow in?

Just turn these distractions off—at least while you are doing something else. There is nothing more certain than a single thought to break a flowing presentation, the creation of a beautiful work of art, or the straight flight of an arrow. Quite simply, multitasking does not work.

Keep It Simple

The reason is that the interruption will have exceeded your seven packets of information. The result is likely to be poor decisions, a sense of energy draining away, and the pleasure of the moment lost forever. Leonardo da Vinci considered simplicity the ultimate sophistication despite being the leading scholar of his time in almost every known discipline.

The problem is that many people believe they can multitask effectively and become rather vociferous when challenged on this subject. Sometimes, they are totally correct. If the tasks are simple and repetitive, they can be safely left to the unconscious and will likely be performed better.

When it is necessary to make important decisions on the basis of complex information, however, concentration is required. This concentration involves the effective mobilization of an exquisite balance of both conscious and unconscious thought.

You will almost certainly be painfully surprised by how hard you find it to turn off all your information-gathering gadgets. When was the last time you turned them off for more than twelve hours? Many people struggle with twelve minutes.

Have you noticed the harassed executives at the hotel reception who are unable to find a Wi-Fi connection in some remote corner of the world? They feel stressed and react illogically because their brains have become addicted to the constant flow of current information, and they feel lost without it. These corporate samurais have convinced themselves that their business is unable to survive without their full 24/7 control.

Of course, they are wrong. And ultimately, they pay a heavy price for their self-delusion, as do the companies that employ them. Their families suffer far more.

Give Your Brain a Holiday

The last few pages gave multiple examples of the distractions that form the barriers to developing mindfulness. The best way to find out just how much the previous comments apply to you is to put them to the test. Indeed, it is the only way. If you have the time and the money, go away for six months. Find some place without Internet, TV, radio, or newspapers—not an easy mission in today's world!

Few except the truly fortunate ones can afford a six-month sabbatical. Many more, however, can manage two weeks, a week, a long weekend, or even just two days. Go ahead and try it. I did, and I found the experience a lot more disturbing than I thought.

Fortunately, the benefits outweighed the losses. At least, I felt a lot healthier, slept deeper and longer, and was much more creative. It took considerably more effort than I anticipated, but it was worth it. Perhaps you might like to take your brain on a holiday where you could both get away for some quality time with each other.

See for yourself. You, too, will sleep better and feel a lot happier. We are all unique and special people. When sensory input is reduced and much of what remains is directly in tune and in alignment with our life goals, the energy will surely flow. Who can guess what other magical things might happen to you?

This chapter has explored the chaotic mess that we call our brain. If it were a trash can, there is no way we could close the lid on it because of its overflowing contents. Much of this garbage is worthless, even though we may not know it. Unfortunately, the precious gold nuggets that hide within this waste may be lost from sight forever. What better time than now for a thorough spring clean? You could do worse than follow K. T. Jong's advice and turn down the volume. Less noise equates to more signal: "It is only when we silent the blaring sounds of our daily existence that we can finally hear the whispers of truth that life reveals to us, as it stands knocking on the doorsteps of our hearts".

The more information you move from the conscious to the unconscious areas of your brain, the higher your performance level will be. This is true for any area of your life, at home, in sports, or at work.

Now review your notes and thoughts on this chapter.

Ask yourself this question: "What three things can I do now that can help me immediately, or at least in the very near future, to make more luck and find more health, wealth, and happiness?"

Write your three points down in the booth. Give yourself sufficient time to digest these thoughts. Some of them might be uncomfortable, because this chapter was about what not to do to become mindful. The next chapter will focus on several far more positive strategies that will be fun and will definitely produce incredible results in some lucky people.

Meditation Booth
Three Nuggets for Now

1.

2.

3.

5

The 3 Hs Of Havening, Heartmath, And Hypnosis

THE THREE Hs of havening, HeartMath, and hypnosis are the most powerful weapons in my armory. These comprise the fifth secret of getting lucky. Used together, they have helped produce some incredible results in my clients. One of the most notable examples is that of a professional poker player who won over $1 million shortly after our sessions together. Another golf client scored three holes-in-one in just six months. The odds against this happening are astronomical.

All three of these techniques have their supporters and skeptics. The science to support each of them is incomplete and sometimes controversial. All I know is that I practice these techniques daily, and they work well for me and my clients, too. Here is a little more information about these techniques.

Havening, HeartMath, and hypnosis have much in common with one another and are closely related to meditation. Where they differ is that meditation is a universal technique that provides an overall calm and focused mind, whereas havening, HeartMath, and hypnosis can be used for specific problems, especially when facilitated by a trained therapist.

Finding a Safe Place

Havening is a new technique that is described as a psychosensory therapy. It uses sensory input to change the neurochemical wiring in a deep part of the brain.

It is particularly effective in treating posttraumatic stress disorders. Threats are perceived through our five senses and enter the thalamus, where they are processed. If perceived as imminently dangerous, they are encoded in the amygdala. An exception is a threat received through the sense of smell. This passes straight to the amygdala. This is presumably an evolutionary shortcut adaptation, as fire may have been the most common direct threat to life in the early ages.

When a frightening event occurs, it is permanently encoded in the amygdala. The amygdala, which can be described as a meerkat, never sleeps and is always alert for potential danger. The problem is that sometimes an event can be perceived as dangerous when, in reality, it is quite trivial. So trivial events in childhood that have been miscoded can exert strong negative influences throughout adult life.

Research has now shown that these traumatic events need not to be permanently encoded. Havening involves remembering the traumatic event and its associated emotional overlay. These emotions include anger, frustration, guilt, shame, jealousy, and frustration.

The therapist strokes the client's face, arms, and hands in a particular way while also performing repeated distraction techniques. Once suitably trained, clients can perform this technique on themselves. The therapeutic result is achieved by a process called receptor depotentiation. In simple terms, this breaks the bond that binds the neurotransmitter to its encoded memory, thus releasing the memory from permanent storage. This is why havening is also known as the amygdala depotentiation technique.

Four elements are required to encode a traumatic memory.

1. Event
2. Meaning
3. Landscape of the brain
4. Perceived inescapability

First, an event must occur. It could be a direct experience, something that we witness, or something we are told or read about. Direct experiences are the most powerful.

Second, the event must have some meaning for the individual. By definition, this would include a powerful emotional component. Most of this meaning arises from experience, although there are some inbuilt fears such as loud noises or being dropped from a height, which even babies feel. Metaphorically, this is because the meerkat is protecting us from danger—real or imagined. The most powerful dangers are those that involve physical or emotional traumatization to ourselves or those we love.

The third element required for traumatization leading to traumatic encoding is the landscape of the brain—in other words, the neurochemical susceptibility of the brain at any one time. For example, the landscape of the brain is particularly vulnerable at times of hormonal imbalance, such as during puberty, menopause, or periods of prolonged stress.

The fourth element required for traumatic encoding is that the event is perceived as inescapable—the feeling of being a vulnerable victim who is powerless to prevent the terrible danger being imposed.

So how does havening work? Dr. Ron Ruden founded the havening technique. I was first introduced to him by self-development guru Paul McKenna and have had the privilege to work with him on many occasions.

Dr. Ruden describes the background to havening far more elegantly and eloquently than I possibly could on page 35 of the training manual he prepared for practitioners preparing for certification. Simply called *Havening—A Manual*, it was published in 2013.

There are three aspects to havening. First, there is the retrieval of the event by imaginal recall. This activates the phosphorylated AMPA receptors that have been encoded at the time of the event. This activation exposes the phosphate molecule that is anchoring the AMPA receptor to the surface of the post-synaptic neuron in the lateral nucleus.

Second, once activated, havening touch, a gentle and soothing touch, is then applied to the upper arms, palms and around the eyes. This touch can be applied either by the therapist or the client. This touch, a comforting, soothing touch produces a unique response of safety that arises as the equivalent of a mother's touch to her newborn baby. The newborn has an innate fear of abandonment that causes it to cry out. The mother whose brain is drenched in the hormone oxytocin (the labor-inducing and human bonding hormone) hears this cry. The sound drives the mother to hold, stroke and comfort her newborn child. The child perceives it is safe, the crying abates and both are comforted. This relationship, between soothing touch and safety, lasts a lifetime.

Thirdly, and concurrently with havening touch there is distraction or chanting. Distraction displaces the recalled event from consciousness and prevents it from continuously activating the amygdala. Generally, this distraction also prevents other distressing thoughts from entering awareness, but not always. Distraction techniques can be visual, auditory or cognitive, such as imagining climbing stairs, humming a tune or counting backward. While the entire process might seem curious, its effects are almost immediate and profound.

Havening is effective in a wide range of neurological disorders including phobias, panic attacks, addictions, and chronic pain.

I use havening with every client, because in the majority of cases, each client has at least one traumatic event that has been encoded. Releasing the fear and emotion from this event is always the first step.

When the client describes the euphoric feeling of letting go, I can then move forward and explore future goals and identify the resources that the client will require to reach them.

There really is no limit to the creativity with which havening can be used, and I use it in a wide variety of circumstances.

In summary, havening is a way to move forward from the past and paint such a vivid picture of the future that the client begins to lead a life of self-fulfilling prophecies.

As mentioned previously, it can be conducted by any appropriately qualified therapist or by the client alone. My preference is always to see a client in person for havening, although I have also reached successful outcomes remotely via Skype.

However, there are times when these options are unavailable, and self-havening is the only viable alternative. While this would be my least-preferred option, it is nevertheless very powerful. The following instructions for self-havening are taken (with minor formatting adaptations) from the havening website.[4]

Self-Havening Instructions

1. Activate the emotional component of the distressing event by bringing it to your mind. If a craving or compulsion is experienced, this is sufficient activation. Rate the distress level from zero to ten, where zero is not at all and ten is extreme. This is called a SUD (subjective units of distress) score.
2. Begin self-havening by applying havening touch to the upper arms; that is, move your hands down the upper arms, circle outward, and repeat downward stroking.
3. At the same time, with your eyes closed, visualize walking up a staircase of twenty steps. As you climb, each step causes the distress, desire, or compulsion to diminish and you to feel safe, peaceful, and calm. Count one to twenty aloud as you climb up the steps in your imagination. Continue arm self-havening.
4. After you have reached twenty, begin to hum a familiar tune while continuing the arm havening. When finished, take a deep breath, open your eyes, and look to the right and left. Close your eyes, inhale deeply, and slowly exhale. Continue arm havening and rate your SUD.

5. Repeat steps two to four with face and palm havening. You may choose the same visual and song, or another for variety. Other visual images can include swimming, running, jumping rope, and so forth. You can then hum a familiar tune of your choice. After each round (arm, face, palm) rate your SUD. Continue until you reach zero or your SUD score remains stable after two additional rounds.

There are numerous instructional videos on YouTube that demonstrate the havening technique. Mothers are often perfect examples to observe when they unconsciously use the havening touch with their children. They did not need to read a book or go through a course to learn this technique. It is a natural reflex to comfort another person.

Finding a Coherent Place

HeartMath is also a relatively new technique and is a form of meditation. The benefits of regular meditation are well established in science. They include reducing anxiety, high blood pressure, and even cancer.

HeartMath is being used increasingly in professional sports and in schools to enhance performance and create the ideal mental state. The heart contains large amounts of nerves. It was thought that these nerves responded to stimulation from the brain. Now it is known that the reverse is often true. The impulses from the heart control the brain.

This might explain why people use the expression, "I knew in my head that this was the right decision, but in my heart I knew it was wrong."

People perform best at work, at school, at sports, or in any creative activity when there is a balance between the challenge of the task and the mental state. If the challenge is low, the mental state is likely to be one of boredom, and so performance will be poor.

If the challenge is balanced in conjunction with a calm mind, then the individual moves into that magical state known as "the zone." This is the home of peak performance.

However, if the challenge is too high, this causes stress and associated loss of confidence. Poor decisions are made because of too many thoughts at one time, and this can result in an increased likelihood of injuries; therefore, any tool that can help a person find the zone more easily and stay there longer will be of immense value. This is exactly what HeartMath delivers when used correctly.

The ideal mental state is dependent on the ability of the individual to strengthen positive emotions and minimize negative ones. Mental state is an incredibly complex balance, with over fourteen hundred known biochemical changes affecting it.

The main hormone associated with negative emotions and, therefore, poor performance is cortisol. These negative emotions include anxiety, frustration, and low confidence. Unless this mind state is changed, it will lead eventually to a cynical approach to life, increasing exhaustion, and, ultimately, acceptance of defeat.

The main hormone that stimulates positive emotions is dehydroepiandrosterone (DHEA). This produces a mind state that is dynamic, confident, and full of passion. Such people are cool under pressure, in control of themselves and their emotions, and calm with a feeling of inner peace.

The core of HeartMath is the perfectly balanced relationship between the heart and the brain. The brain is packed with nerve cells, which is why it controls the rest of the body with perfect precision.

What is less known is that there are also numerous nerve cells in and around the heart. Even lesser known is the stunning fact that these nerve cells from the heart send more information to the brain than the other way round; therefore, the brain is not controlling the heart, but the heart is controlling the brain. Using this knowledge, you can apply the HeartMath technique to enhance your mental state and hence promote peak performance.

At the core of the HeartMath technique is the concept of "heart-rate variability." For example, if your heart rate is sixty, then that means that your heart must beat once every second. However, it is not quite as simple as that because during any five-second period, the heart may beat five times. But it is also quite likely that it may beat only four times, or as many as six times. So the heart rate is only an average number of beats in a sixty-second period. This variation between individual heartbeats is called the "heart-rate variability."

Heart-rate variability is dependent upon our age, general state of health, and, most important, our mental state. High heart-rate variability produces positive emotions, while the opposite is true of low heart variability.

So how can we increase our heart-rate variability and find the ideal mental state known as coherence? The answer is to practice specific breathing techniques. These techniques, which lead to a slightly higher level of coherence, are very simple, and yet they still produce great benefit.

There are also more complex HeartMath techniques, some of which are computerized. They are particularly helpful because they provide a second-by-second recording of your mental state. Even though I have practiced them every day for many years, I am still learning how to achieve greater coherence scores.

The following breathing technique is a great way to start to understand how to use HeartMath. We have already stressed the importance of the heart. So to start this exercise, bring your attention to the area around your heart. Then breathe rhythmically and at the same time imagine that your breath is going into and then leaving your heart.

Breathe in for five seconds, and breathe out for five seconds. Perform this exercise for five minutes, or even less, and you will feel much calmer.

The truth is that it is very difficult to be calm when you are breathing quickly; it is even more difficult to be anxious when you are breathing slowly.

I have mentioned many times the importance of the emotions to our state of mind. So your next challenge is to use the simple technique described earlier, but add another magic ingredient to the mix—a positive emotion. Think of a person you love and who loves you. Think of a time when life was easy and you were in the zone performing at a much higher level than normal. Think of how you would like to feel in the future, and the goals you would like to achieve in your life. Then think of how good this will make you feel.

While you are generating these positive emotions and chemicals, focus your mind at the same time on the feeling of breathing through your heart. Just as before, breathe in for five seconds, and breathe out for five seconds.

This technique is very useful in reproducing past emotional highs that we can then use for future events that we might find threatening.

The HeartMath Institute has an extremely informative website, and much of its content is freely available. It is well worth a visit. This is a brief summary of HeartMath adapted from the institute's website:[5]

- Thoughts and even subtle emotions influence the activity and balance of the autonomic nervous system (ANS).
- The ANS interacts with our digestive, cardiovascular, immune, and hormonal systems.
- Negative reactions create disorder and imbalance in the ANS.
- Positive feelings, such as appreciation, create increased order and balance in the ANS, which results in increased hormonal and immune-system balance and more efficient brain function.
- A growing body of compelling scientific evidence is demonstrating the link between mental and emotional attitudes, physiological health, and long-term well-being.

In addition, these are some of the more compelling HeartMath research findings, published in the booklet *Science of the Heart* on page 10, and provide much food for thought.[6]

A Harvard Medical School study of 1,623 heart-attack survivors found that when subjects became angry during emotional conflicts, their risk of subsequent heart attacks was more than double that of those who remained calm.

Men who complain of high anxiety are up to six times more likely than calmer men to suffer sudden cardiac death.

A twenty-year study of over seventeen hundred older men conducted by the Harvard School of Public Health found that worry about social conditions, health, and personal finances all significantly increased the risk of heart disease.

Over one-half of heart-disease cases are not explained by standard risk factors such as high cholesterol, smoking, or sedentary lifestyle.

An international study of 2,829 people between the ages of fifty-five and eighty-five found that individuals who reported the highest levels of personal "mastery"—feelings of control over life events—had a nearly 60 percent lower risk of death compared with those who felt relatively helpless in the face of life's challenges.

According to a Mayo Clinic study of individuals with heart disease, psychological stress was the strongest predictor of future cardiac events, such as cardiac death, cardiac arrest, and heart attacks.

Three ten-year studies concluded that emotional stress was more predictive of death from cancer and cardiovascular disease than smoking. People who were unable to effectively manage their stress had a 40 percent higher death rate than unstressed individuals.

A recent study of heart-attack survivors showed that emotional state and relationships of patients in the period after myocardial infarction are as important as the disease severity in determining their prognosis.

In a study of 5,716 middle-aged people, those with the highest self-regulation abilities were over fifty times more likely to be alive and without chronic disease fifteen years later than those with the lowest self-regulation scores.

So the message is clear. HeartMath is a form of meditation that anyone can practice. As the benefits are now beyond dispute, any form of meditation is well worth your further consideration.

Finding a Deep Place

The third of these H techniques is hypnosis. Indeed it is often referred to as the "H word," because it has such negative connotations among some people. I do not fully understand why this is so, but perhaps there needs to be a clearer distinction between stage hypnosis and the therapeutic hypnosis that I practice. I have never used hypnosis other than as a psychotherapeutic intervention.

We are surrounded by examples of hypnosis, and everybody can be a hypnotist. One of the best examples is the natural way that a mother soothes her troubled child. Many commercials that we see on TV are also hypnotic, irrespective of whether their creators know this.

I can guarantee one thing: you will be confused by hypnosis. If you are a hypnotist, if you are hypnotized, or if you are a student of hypnosis, the more you study hypnosis, the more confused you will become. I can only hope that it is confusion at a deeper level of understanding.

I have already mentioned that hypnosis forms the foundation of my work with clients. I am considered to be an excellent hypnotist, particularly by the legendary self-help guru Paul McKenna. He should know, because much of what I learned, I learned from him. We now work together quite often, and I am still learning. I know from our conversations that Paul is, too.

I have probably been a hypnotist all my life. I experimented on my mother when I was a teenager, and she had such a strong reaction that I was too terrified to hypnotize another person for many years. I now know that this reaction is called an "abreaction" and is a relatively common occurrence. With the wisdom of twenty-twenty retrospective hindsight, I can categorically state that no one should hypnotize another person unless he or she is confident and competent in his or her ability to handle an abreaction.

In 2007, my career was at a crossroads. I could have carried on in the same direction and led a very comfortable life, but I was paying the price of becoming increasingly bored.

The alternative was that I was young enough to start a new career in the subject that has always fascinated me—psychology. I was, however, not young enough to go back to university and earn another master's degree, let alone have enough time to build a client base.

I needed accelerated learning, and the best way to learn fast is to study with the best. You cannot do much better than to train with Richard Bandler and Paul McKenna, as both are regarded as world experts in their field.

I have tried to read books about hypnosis but have never finished one. I find them incomprehensible. Hypnosis is something you learn from doing, although under close supervision. You do not learn these skills from books.

Even now, I do not know how I produce the results that I do. All I know is that I become aware when I enter the altered mental state known as "hypnosis." I also know when my clients do, too, which is usually shortly after me. It is also a lot earlier than the client expects. A common expression among fellow therapists is that "one has to go there first."

According to the books, hypnosis is induced by a series of preliminary instructions and suggestions. These can be lengthy and complicated, and I have seen some hypnotists even reading their induction script from a detailed checklist.

I can only give my opinion, and I apologize if it contradicts other views that may be equally valid or even more so. I do not, however, use hypnotic inductions. The nearest I come to a formal induction is to sit quietly in meditation without speaking for a few minutes before starting to talk to my client.

Light hypnosis can be achieved within seconds, and deep hypnosis within another minute or two. It is not necessary to reach a state of deep hypnosis to perform deep hypnotherapy. Sometimes even a light trance produces more spectacular results. Hypnosis should be seen as an as art and used sparingly.

I do not know how hypnosis works its magic. But I do know that it is a deeply relaxing or meditative state of mind, whereby the busy conscious mind is quieted so that the deeper thoughts from the unconscious mind can surface.

I do not know in what area of the brain hypnosis produces its effects either. There is increasing evidence that suggests that the nerve cells of the brain are "plastic." In other words, these cells are malleable; for example, cells normally devoted to vision can change their function. In a blind person, the cells may become sound receptor cells so that they can provide a different sensory input to aid the person.

Complex new neural pathways are being created and destroyed all the time. Sooner or later the network reaches its optimum route, and a process called "myelination" kicks in. An example would be a child learning to ride a bike. Most of the early neural pathways result in the child falling off the bike until something magical connects. After this, the child will remember to ride a bike for the rest of his or her life and do so without even consciously thinking about it.

I do not believe that hypnosis is dangerous when performed by a competent therapist or that there are some people who cannot be hypnotized. If there are, then I have not met them.

I believe that some people who are determined to resist hypnosis will do so very effectively; however, sooner or later, their resistance will wear down. But by then, the hypnotist will also be so exhausted that it will not make any difference.

Perhaps hypnosis works its magic by establishing communication with the deeper layers of the brain. This makes it possible to learn skills much faster than when using willpower and traditional methods of coaching.

Even when I considered myself a competent hypnotist, I struggled with self-hypnosis. I felt that this would be an important skill to learn because legend has it that it is incredibly beneficial to live life in a light trance. And so it has been proven. I spend hours in light trance, but then so do many other people. The difference is that I know when I'm in a trance and can use it productively, whereas others might not and will have missed out on the opportunity to use it well.

Another very interesting aspect of hypnosis is that it has frequently been considered a possible military interrogation tool.

A US study, *Hypnosis in Intelligence*, was published in October 1966 and declassified in September 2000. It left the researchers predictably confused.[7]

"It would be difficult to find an area of scientific interest more beset by divided professional opinion and contradictory experimental evidence…No one can say whether hypnosis is a qualitatively unique state with some physiological and conditioned response components or only a form of suggestion induced by high motivation and a positive relationship between hypnotist and subject."

So for the foreseeable future, hypnosis will raise more questions than answers; however, it is certain that its effects can be very powerful and very beneficial. It is a subject worth further consideration in your journey to attract more luck into your life.

Havening, HeartMath, and hypnosis are much easier to talk about, or see in action, than read about. You'll see further information on how to get started on this in the conclusion.

Now review your notes and thoughts on this chapter.

Ask yourself this question: "What three things can I do now that can help me immediately, or at least in the very near future, to make more luck and find more health, wealth, and happiness?"

Write your three points down in the booth.

If this chapter was not confusing enough, the next chapter will examine luck from several other different angles. Some of these will be eminently sensible, while others will border on the absurd.

One thing is certain: Its conclusions will raise at least a niggling question in your mind about whether we truly live in a totally random universe.

Meditation Booth
Three Nuggets for Now

1.

2.

3.

6

The Luck Magnet

THE SIXTH SECRET to getting lucky is luck itself. Or, more precisely, it is how you can attract more luck into your life by being a luck magnet. Is this possible?

The truth is that it is possible, and there are some logical reasons for this. We will cover some of these in this chapter.

Supporters claim that there are also some extremely illogical reasons that can attract luck. These are more difficult to explain and will be covered in the next chapter.

I spoke to many people about luck while researching this book. An expression that I heard often was: "The harder I work, the luckier I get."

This is true, because everything in life has to be worked at. Very few people achieve great success without a considerable effort, yet many spend their whole lives working very hard but with little luck and success to show for it, compared with those who work a lot less and are lot luckier.

You Do Not Need to Spend Ten Years in Day Jail, Though It Helps

In conversation and in print, I have often come across the theory of ten thousand hours. Apparently, it takes at least ten thousand hours of deep practice to become an expert at anything.

Without doubt, there is a lot of truth in this statement. But it is quoted as if this is the whole truth, when nothing could be further from it. The reason this statement worries me is that it can be a powerful, negative self-fulfilling prophecy. It also does not give enough credit to innate talent or to the power of accelerated learning delivered by skillful coaching.

How many people will be thrown off learning a new skill when they figure that ten thousand hours of deep practice will take them at least ten years to clock?

The ten-thousand-hour story surfaced in a paper published by K. Anders Ericsson and his colleagues in 1993. It is a brilliant paper, forty-four pages long, extremely technical, and definitely not an easy read, which might be why the conclusions are not as clear as some might believe. When writing a scientific paper, the biggest challenge for the author is to eliminate what statisticians call "confounding factors." These can skew the results and lead to faulty conclusions.

Let me explain. Do you think that a kid who clocks ten thousand hours of deep violin practice is going to be the average kid next door, who has average parents with an average income and an average interest in music?

I don't think so. And, to be fair, neither did Ericsson and his colleagues. They were the first to accept that their elegant paper raised a lot more questions than answers. Of course this talented and conscientious kid wholly deserves our respect. But I'm more interested in the kid from the ghetto who does not have these advantages, but who improvises and finds other ways that allow talent to surface—the kid who has fun, experiments, but does not take ten thousand hours to be an expert.

Do as They Do

More good news in our search for luck reveals that researchers have identified a consistent pattern among people who lead a lucky life. They are often extroverted and hence attract many friends. They have large social networks and are often the first to hear of new opportunities. They are social magnets, and because of this, they are luck magnets, too. This is unlikely to be a coincidence.

Another characteristic of lucky people is that they have a relaxed attitude to life and are more likely to see all of the options available to them in any situation. This is in stark contrast to anxious people who have their focus on internal, rather than external, issues, and so never recognize these opportunities.

Lucky people also have more open minds, and this seems to be particularly important. Often, they share an unconventional outlook on life as well. This is probably not too surprising. Success and luck are inextricably linked, and successful people often identify their strength as seeing unusual opportunities that others do not.

Others miss them because these opportunities do not fit the pattern that they expect to see. This is the same reason why most people struggle to spot a hologram on the first occasion. After initial processing, the visual cortex rejects the hologram because it is so different from a normal image. This rejection occurs because the image does not fit the expected and well-developed innate pattern-recognition criteria that we all possess.

Conversely, cynical people are usually not lucky people. Luckily for me, the majority of my clients are not cynical. This is probably because they are a self-selected group. Most people do not take the time and trouble to find a mind coach, so my clients are not a representative cross-sectional sample. This is another example of a confounding factor, just like the musician mentioned earlier.

While they are not cynical, some do have doubts when we start to work together. Are they good enough to succeed? Are my techniques good enough? Am I good enough?

I fully understand these doubts and am aware that there will be an underlying reason for these to have surfaced. So I explore their past experiences and usually identify a small number of incidents that have disproportionately colored their outlook on life.

Then I can focus on techniques that remind clients of all the great things that they have achieved and the wonderful people they have met. This allows them to put into perspective their previous bad experiences and the people who let them down. I then move on, and these clients do at least as well as the others.

In a previous chapter, we talked about visualization, and we know that lucky people definitely have big dreams. Some of these big dreams will never be realized, and the cynics will enjoy pointing this out to them; however, some of these dreams will come true because the more often you position yourself for success, the more likely it is that you will succeed at some point.

Another pitfall to avoid is being too content after a lucky experience. Good luck materializing out of the blue can be frightening to some people. On occasions, it has been frightening for me, too. So I can understand why they should feel this way.

A common expression such people use is "I'm going to take it easy now because I don't want to push my luck too far."

However, when lucky people are on a roll, they don't stop riding the wave. They keep having their big dreams and fully expect their good luck to continue in the future. Even in adverse situations, they truly believe that it is only a matter of time before the tide will turn and their luck will change with it.

However, even lucky people face adversity at some point in their life, and, once again, their attitude toward it is very different than that of unlucky people. Lucky people are convinced that however bad things may be now, all will work out for the best in the future. They truly feel that they will be stronger for the experience. They do not blame themselves or others for their misfortune and move on to the future far more rapidly than do most people. The unlucky people, however, give up in the face of adversity—sometimes when they are a lot closer to their goal than they realize.

Good Luck or Bad Luck?

You may have heard of bad luck–good luck stories. I am going to share my story with you and then ask you to write down your story, too. It will almost certainly be very illuminating.

I have been lucky throughout my life and can only remember three occasions when luck deserted me. In comparison to many people's experiences, these misfortunes are somewhat trivial. But at the time, they were extremely stressful.

My first bad experience was in 1990. Everything was going well in my life. The years of long hours and hard work I spent gaining qualifications were behind me, and I had just been awarded my first senior position. I was appointed the medical director for a major multinational corporation.

The job had an attractive salary and all the other good things, including the share options that went with it. Like many people my age, I had young children to support and a sizable mortgage as well. While I was lucky to be awarded this job, my timing was extremely unlucky.

England was in the depths of a major recession and interest rates were rising, making the monthly mortgage payments difficult. In less than a year, the company I was working for collapsed, leaving me without a job and bills to pay. I knew that it would be difficult to find any work, never mind discovering a job of my dreams.

As I had been working abroad for several years, my network of contacts was limited. I called a few people, and as I had expected, the responses were not promising. There was one potential lead, though. The position was based in London and consisted largely of performing executive medical examinations. While such examinations are important, I found performing them dreary. Another problem was that there was another shortlisted candidate. I would only be interviewed if he turned down the job.

To cut a long story short, he turned the job down, and I took it out of desperation. I cannot say that I enjoyed it, but it paid the bills and allowed me to sleep at night. Then I got lucky again.

The new company I was working for had major operations in Africa and was finding it increasingly difficult to recruit people with the skills it needed. The main barrier to recruitment was the poor medical facilities available for the employee and his or her family. At one point, more than half of the expatriates and their families had been admitted to the Hospital for Tropical Diseases in London.

Company officials knew they had to find an answer to this recruitment problem because it was critical for their success in hiring sufficient people with the skills they needed. A task force was assembled to study the medical issues and prepare a report with recommendations to address this issue.

I was invited to be a member of this study team. As I should have guessed, I was soon offered the job of implementing the recommendations that we had prepared, and I had to move to Nigeria with my family.

I quickly found out that it was one thing to propose a plan and quite another to deliver it. The following years went by in a blur. This was a very happy time, with many wonderful memories that will last a lifetime, despite being mugged, imprisoned, shot at, shelled, almost killed in a helicopter incident, and experiencing near-fatal malaria, dengue fever, dysentery, and the dubious delights of tumbu infection.

I continued working for the same company for the next seventeen years in Nigeria, Kazakhstan, and Angola. Little did I know then that I would be right at the heart of the battle against HIV in Africa. Not even in my wildest dreams could I have imagined that I would have the privilege to work with many world leaders, including Bill Clinton, nor could I have known that I would work as a task-force member of the World Economic Forum and Global Business Coalition.

This is my first bad luck–good luck story, and it took longer than I expected to write it. So I will not bore you with the details of my other two bad luck–good luck stories. These will wait for another time.

This is a good time for you to contemplate your bad luck–good luck stories. The time spent may be richly rewarded.

When the Going Gets Tough, the Tough Get Going

The next section in this chapter is equally important and describes the importance of adversity—or more accurately, how we handle it.

This is important because lucky people are able to handle adversity much better than most people. They always see the positive side and bounce back, often remarking that things could have been a lot worse and that they had been really lucky to escape.

Lucky people really do look on the bright side of life, and you might even remember these words of the song made famous by Monty Python. Perhaps even now it will bring a smile to your lips.

Adversity is a serious subject and extremely important in determining whether you will be a luck magnet. It is not a topic we like to think about too much, but it is how we deal with it that determines our level of happiness (or lack thereof) and whether we will attract luck.

As always, it is well worth studying other people to find answers for ourselves. Specifically study those individuals who were able to triumph over adversity. It is a rare gift to be able to turn a negative situation into a positive one. This is why society quite rightly admires survivors. These are people who beat the odds. We all like to see proof that sometimes the odds can be beaten, and if they can do it, then perhaps so can we.

These are the people who made their own luck from nothing, which is just about the greatest skill a person can have.

It Is Good to Be Nice, But Not Too Nice

Dr. Lydia Temoshok is a professor of virology at the University of Maryland Cancer Center. Her career has focused on the relationship between the mind and physical illness. She studied AIDS patients, specifically those who survived much longer than expected—the people who beat the odds.

She also studied melanoma patients. Melanoma is a potentially serious form of skin cancer. Dr. Temoshok researched the characteristics of those individuals who appeared more likely to develop cancer. Her conclusions are remarkably consistent. In her book The Type C Connection she describes the cancer patients as usually being extremely nice people.

> What they shared was a manner of handling life stress. The melanoma patients coped by keeping their feelings under wraps. They never expressed anger, and rarely did they acknowledge fear and

sadness. They maintained a façade of pleasantness even under the most painful or aggravating circumstances. They strived excessively to please people they cared about, to please authority figures, even to please strangers.

But my study of the melanoma patients led me to convincing evidence that our physical health is compromised when we chronically repress our needs and feelings to accommodate others.

We would all like others to think of us as nice people, but perhaps we should not be too nice when fighting cancer.

Dr. Temoshok's research with Dr. George Solomon in 1987 again approached the interaction between the mind and body from a positive perspective. This time they focused on the long-term AIDS survivors rather than those patients more likely to develop skin cancer. They were able to identify the following eight characteristics that correlated with survival:

1. They are realistic and accept their diagnosis and do not take it as a death sentence.
2. They have a fighting spirit and refuse to be helpless or hopeless.
3. They have changed lifestyles.
4. They are assertive and able to get out of stressful and unproductive situations.
5. They are tuned into their own psychological and physical needs, and they take care of them.
6. They are able to talk openly about their illness.
7. They have a sense of personal responsibility for their health and look at the treating health-care provider as a collaborator.
8. They are altruistically involved with other persons with HIV.

Like it or not, we will all face adversity and illness at some point in our lives—sudden sickness, redundancy, poor housing conditions, limited income, work stress, and more. Whatever the situation, there are some role-model behaviors that we can call upon if needed. One of the irritating clichés people use is, "Don't worry, good will come from adversity."

They mean well, but these do not feel like helpful comments at the time; however, when we look back, they are often right. Just like the bad luck–good luck story, very few great successes in life happen easily. They are mostly preceded by months or years of increasing frustration. Another often-heard cliché is, "It was hard to believe at the time, but it was probably the best thing that ever happened to me!"

A similar comment was made centuries ago by Quintus Horatius Flaccus, one of the leading Roman poets at the time of Augustus: "Adversity has the effect of eliciting talents that, in prosperous circumstances, would have lain dormant."

Now review your notes and thoughts on this chapter.

Ask yourself this question: "What three things can I do now that can help me immediately, or at least in the very near future, to make more luck and find more health, wealth, and happiness?"

Write your three points down in the booth.

This chapter explored why some people are lucky and tried to unravel the thread of logic that connected these thin strands of evidence. These same strands will be tested to their limits in the next chapter as we explore the world of the unknown unknowns. Prepare yourself for a bumpy ride.

Meditation Booth
Three Nuggets for Now

1.

2.

3.

7

Magic

The previous chapter focused on the direct-line-of-sight logic that explains why some people have more luck than others. All we have to do is do what they do, and we will attract more luck, too.

As promised, in this chapter we will look at far more esoteric origins of luck. Whether we will be able to use them is less certain, but it is possible. For want of a better word, I call this subject "magic." One definition of "magic" is "the power of apparently influencing events by using mysterious or supernatural forces."

Throughout generations, people have wanted to believe in luck and explain its origin. It is not clear why, but one plausible explanation is that it arises from a deep fear of living in an environment where the individual has little control over external events. Is this fear of the future programmed into our genes? Or is it a behavior that we learned from others and from our own experience?

The answer is probably a combination of all. A certain amount of foresight and planning for the future would give humans an edge over other species in terms of survival. We are warm-blooded and do not possess hide or hair as other creatures do, nor do we need to prepare for the cold months.

At a conscious level, we identify what we want to control in our life. If we cannot or do not wish to exert this control ourselves, we find others to do so by proxy. We have evolved as social animals, and this badge influences almost all our behavior and thoughts.

For example, gamblers believe that they can exert a measure of control over the future, and it forms part of the hook of their addiction. However, gamblers are also convinced that they do not need luck to smile upon their good fortune. They are certain that their system will be more than a match for the law of averages.

Gamblers spend countless hours searching for elaborate patterns from past results. They believe that these patterns will predict future events. Sometimes they are sure that they have found the secret. Yet often, the results they study are only random scatter. A run of winning results brings a euphoric emotional high and can be addictive. Enjoying the sense of mastery over external events is heady stuff, and it is not only gamblers who have fallen prey to its beguiling nature.

This Is the Answer

History is littered with stories of charismatic men and women who promised such control—the promise that order could arise from chaos. Religion attempted to provide answers and meaning, too. Hence the common strand of myths, legends, revelations, and holy scriptures that are shared by many religions.

Philosophers rushed to join the party, and some even challenged the validity of the basic human need for any kind of control. Some insisted that we do not need it and should not waste time and energy searching for it.

Scientists provided their answers, too—often with far more conviction than the facts deserved. Throughout history, philosophers, scientists, artists, and religious leaders have been frequently locked in a titanic struggle for intellectual dominance.

Despite all the fevered rhetoric, however, this struggle has continued for centuries and will likely go on for many more. Renowned astrophysicist Stephen Hawking, however, is convinced that science "doesn't need God" and has already won this battle, with the result that no additional explanation is required by philosophy or religion.

Whether or not he is right, it is not likely that this was a struggle that Mohandas Gandhi would have enjoined. His efforts were focused on living in the moment. Again, this surfaces as the foundation of the fourth secret, mindfulness, as highlighted by his following words.

"I do not want to foresee the future. I am concerned with taking care of the present. God has given me no control over the moment following."

All in Good Time

Now might be a good time to delve even deeper into the esoteric origins of luck. Psychologist Carl Jung viewed luck as "synchronicity," a word that he introduced. He described luck as a meaningful coincidence. So he believed that luck is not random, as do the gamblers. This is very different from Noah Webster's classic dictionary definition of luck, which is "a purposeless unpredictable and uncontrollable force that shapes events favorably or unfavorably for an individual, group, or cause."

Jung was so fascinated by synchronicity that he wrote a paper about it in the 1920s but only published it in 1951, possibly because he knew how controversial it would be. Jung even held long conversations with Albert Einstein about the possible connection between synchronicity and the theory of relativity, as well as quantum mechanics.

Jung felt that his thoughts about synchronicity proved the existence of the collective unconscious. In other words, unrelated events that at first sight appear to be coincidental are in fact related because they draw upon the totality of human experience through the ages.

His views have many dissenters who propose alternative conclusions. Their explanations of synchronicity include the failure of our pattern-recognition skills.

This is a skill that primates have taken to the highest level in their ability to recognize tiny differences between people's faces; therefore, sometimes we can convince ourselves that a pattern exists in a data series when in reality any such pattern is either coincidental or nonexistent.

Others believe that synchronicity is no more than highly developed intellectual intuition. For what it is worth, this is the explanation that I am most comfortable with, especially because there is much that we can do to improve our intuition. All of the secrets of success that I have described in this book can develop your intuition skills.

Often people talk about having gut feelings; lucky people tend to follow them. Most people's conscious minds are so busy that there is no way for the unconscious mind to speak and be heard. So I spend a lot of time with my clients teaching them meditation skills and techniques such as hypnosis, havening, and HeartMath, as mentioned previously.

Yet More Rules

Universal laws, which have many supporters, provide another explanation. Many people now talk about universal laws—especially the law of attraction—as the ultimate form of control. This law proposes that our conscious and unconscious thoughts can influence external events. The best-selling documentary *The Secret* describes the law of attraction in more detail. It was released in 2006 and became instantly popular. Rightly or wrongly, the belief that "thoughts become things" has resonated deeply with millions around the world.

The Secret instructs us that all we have to do is "ask, believe, and receive" and let the power of the universe take care of everything else. For some people, this is enough information, and they are probably already following this or a similar mantra. Others will surely require more convincing. What possible explanation can they be given? If there is an answer, it is most likely hidden deep within the unconscious mind.

The law of attraction instructs us that positive people attract other positive people to them. This is not too surprising. We all know people we like to be with, either at work or in our personal life.

We also know many people who we do not choose to be around. Such people are the habitual moaners who see the worst in any given situation. They are energy vampires and are best avoided. They attract their own circle of like-minded negative thinkers. In extreme cases, because of their focus on negative emotions such as paranoia, jealousy, and anger, their energy can be destructive.

The law of attraction not only postulates that positive people attract other positive people to them, but it says also that positive events attract further positive events. Indeed, the law goes even further and proposes that positive thoughts can lead directly to positive events, even at considerable distances. If even a fraction of this statement is to be believed, then the implications are immense.

Believers use their own models to describe the law of attraction, but the consistent message is that energy follows our thoughts. In some way, this energy expands to influence the event that was the focus of our original intention.

Many grounded and pragmatic people who have never even heard of the law of attraction, let alone put it into practice, believe some strange force is out there, working in their favor. The words they use include "luck," "coincidence," "synchronicity," "serendipity," "fate," and "karma." They explain that a particular event was meant to be, or that things just fell into place.

French surgeon Alexis Carrel won the Nobel Prize for medicine in 1912. His techniques for rejoining blood vessels are still used in transplant surgery to this day. Surgery is by necessity a practical specialty, but Carrel was a controversial freethinker, too. He also believed that unseen forces can shape our destiny. He specifically mentioned intuition, a subject that has surfaced many times in this book already. In the introduction I wrote, "The overarching conclusion I reached writing this book was that luck is inextricably linked to intuition."

I wonder if that is what Carrel had in mind when he wrote, "Intuition comes very close to clairvoyance; it appears to be the extrasensory perception of reality."

Show Me the Money

These ideas are not original, and similar theories were proposed by Napoleon Hill in his book *Think and Grow Rich*. This book was published in 1937 and is still a best seller, with over sixty million copies sold. At least, it worked for Hill. Many of its readers were convinced that it worked for them, too.

Scientists now broadly accept the huge influence and power of the unconscious mind, and yet their research has not even begun to scratch the tip of this iceberg, indeed not even the uppermost ice crystal. On the one hand this is frustrating, but on the other hand, it means that your opinion is just about as valid as anybody else's. Perhaps the law of attraction is yet another example of the unseen power of the unconscious mind.

As mentioned previously, the foundation of *The Secret* is to ask, believe, and receive. What do these words mean?

Perhaps asking is no more than the vivid visualization of our list of skillfully constructed objectives. Others might name such a list as affirmations, or more simply as a wish list. To the unconscious mind, the distinction between reality and perception is blurred. In an earlier chapter, we addressed the importance of visualization, so there should be no surprises here.

Believing is just that. It takes a leap of faith and requires an open mind. Most of us have been persuaded over the years to believe that success comes only from hard work and that practice makes perfect. If something sounds too good to be true, then it is too good to be true.

All of these statements are true most of the time, but not always. How do some people float through life with smiles on their faces, are very successful, and make it all look so easy?

It is because they have found ways to increase their luck. They are good at asking, and they are able to believe in their eventual success, too.

Receiving is also a tricky concept to explain. Sometimes it is easier to give a gift to another than to receive one yourself. The law of attraction requests that we watch for signs and interpret the events around us within the context of what we have asked for. That reception is an active process, not a passive one. Receiving is not waiting for the universe to tap you on the shoulder with a wonderful gift. The gift is already out there waiting for you; you just have to find it.

We already know how we all miss a huge amount of vital information that is right in front of us—information that could change our lives. More accurately, we do not miss this information; we just fail to process it from our unconscious into our conscious mind. Or our processing is incomplete, which may lead to critical errors of interpretation.

Our mind takes multiple huge shortcuts and largely "sees" what it expects to see, on the basis of previous experiences. This is why it is so difficult to see a hologram for the first time. The image is there and processed accurately by the visual pathway, yet it is rejected by the higher brain centers because it does not fit the expected pattern.

When we see, hear, or feel something that is so unusual that our conscious mind rejects it, the echo of this memory still persists. It causes a feeling of uneasiness, similar to the irritation of an unfinished conversation, until it finds the right environment to surface—often annoyingly at four in the morning when we are struggling to sleep.

Receiving is possibly another example of intuition, and like any other skill, it can be improved with practice. Poet and author Robert Graves knew its value: "Intuition is the supra-logic that cuts out all the routine processes of thought and leaps straight from the problem to the answer."

So how can you use all this contradictory and confusing information? Be prepared to experiment with different options. It is not likely that success will arise from repeating previous unsuccessful efforts. Indeed, Einstein had defined insanity as doing the same thing repeatedly and expecting different results.

Trust your intuition and instincts but always ask yourself, "What is the risk?" This is the safety net, because while instincts are often proven to be correct, there are occasions when they can be spectacularly misplaced, and with dire consequences.

Whether or not you can accept the possibility that the law of attraction can work for you, why not try it and see? Within the context of attempting to identify the ingredients of personal happiness, the truth is that living life with a positive attitude has got to be a lot more fun than expecting everything to go wrong. This is sometimes described as the glass-half-full mind-set, as opposed to the glass-half-empty.

Howard Schultz, CEO of Starbucks, believes we make our own luck by our own efforts, without the need for a mystical explanation: "I believe life is a series of near misses. A lot of what we ascribe to luck is not luck at all. It's seizing the day and accepting responsibility for your future. It's seeing what other people don't see and pursuing that vision."

Self-development guru Paul McKenna also believes we create our own luck and studies successful people to identify their secrets. He writes, "Whether you choose to believe in the law of attraction or not, it's interesting to note that many highly successful people do."

So these ideas merit further reflection, irrespective of their current lack of scientific basis. The law of attraction has provided lucky breaks for many of its supporters and just might do the same for you, too.

Is there a contradiction here? Surely, the law of attraction is about thinking of the future and what we want. Yet we have already considered the importance of staying in the present. How can both arguments be valid?

A possible explanation for this disconnect is that the law of attraction considers the future to have already occurred. You have made your wish, and there is little more that you can do to fulfill it apart from staying in the present, doing the best job you can, and waiting. What will be will be.

There Is Nothing to Worry About

If you are not comfortable with universal laws, perhaps the world of science might have something more persuading to explain how luck might not be random. You will be the judge, so here goes.

According to quantum physics, all matter is made of almost completely nothing, and so are you. The majority of what appears to be a rock, airplane, or even a person is really just empty space surrounded by a small amount of matter.

Almost everything in the universe is nothing. If you could extract all the matter from our population, it would just about cover your thumbnail. Everything else is nothing—just empty space between the smallest subatomic particles. It is rather like staring up into the sky on a clear night, where the stars are the equivalent of our subatomic particles and the rest is empty space.

In one sense, however, this space is not empty. Energy travels through it. This energy includes gravitational effects from stars. It also includes radio waves and radiation and all the other components of the electromagnetic spectrum. The only part of the spectrum you perceive is the tiny bit you can see, which is the visible light.

The two greatest breakthroughs in physics during the last century were the advances in the theories of relativity and quantum mechanics. Leading physicist Stephen Hawking writes in *A Briefer History of Time*, "Today scientists describe the universe, in terms of two basic partial theories, the general theory of relativity and quantum mechanics."

Relativity concerns very large objects, whereas quantum theory is about very small ones. A quantum is the smallest discrete quantity of a physical property, such as electromagnetic radiation or angular momentum.

Quantum physics is the study of energy and matter and their complex relationships. Many eminent scientists were and continue to be excited by quantum theory, particularly because it opened considerable debate about actual reality, perceived reality, and the blurry area in between.

So what does this have to do with luck? Perhaps it has nothing to do with luck at all, or perhaps it just might. Right or wrong, quantum theory has been used to explain the blurry area between our perception of reality, where the power of the mind could produce an effect on matter. It is also the area where both ancient and modern philosophies meet science head on.

Who Let the Cat Out?

Some top athletes openly talk about the benefits that their thinking around quantum theory has brought to their game. Rugby Union star Jonny Wilkinson described a breakthrough in his fight against his fear of not achieving his goals when reading about the quantum thought experiment known as Schrödinger's cat.

Schrödinger sought to illustrate quantum theory by imagining a cat in a sealed box with a jar of cyanide and a piece of radioactive material. There is a 50 percent chance, at a given time, that the material has decayed enough to trigger the release of the poison. At that time, quantum physics says, the cat is both alive and dead; however, as soon as one opens the box, the cat is either alive or dead.

"It had a huge effect on me," Wilkinson said. "The idea that an observer can change the world just by looking at it, the idea that the mind and reality are somehow interconnected...it hit me like a steam train."

Not surprisingly, this blurry area has also attracted more than its share of controversy. At its extreme interpretation, any event that is unexplainable can be attributed to quantum physics in action. This is very convenient, because such a statement cannot be proved false.

It is not only athletes who subscribe to the benefits that quantum theory promises; some of the scientists who coach and study them do, too. Gottfried Mayer-Kress put forward some extremely compelling ideas in his keynote conference presentation to the 2001 International Sports Coaching Symposium of the Chinese Taipei University Sports Federation, in Taichung, Taiwan.[8]

Since quantum computation seems to be a macroscopic reality, it would be very surprising if natural evolution would not have developed means to exploit this computational resource that could give our biological brains—running more than a million times slower than today's notebook computers—the impressive computational capabilities that we observe in today's athletes. In terms of physical processes it is also clear that the microscopic events that lead to a decision to activate (or not activate) certain muscles during a movement process are fundamentally of a quantum nature, namely the electro-chemical processes in nerve membranes.

Could this be a possible explanation of how advanced visualization techniques enhance performance?

Quantum physics is by far the most complex subject I have ever researched. The only reason that I include it in a book about luck, although with considerable trepidation, is because it is a subject of increasingly common debate. It just might explain how some people seem able to control their lives more skillfully and achieve more success than others. Perhaps quantum physics forms the magical energy behind the law of attraction.

Hawking, too, shares Einstein's belief that a new theory will one day unify the theories of relativity and quantum physics. He calls this a quantum theory of gravity. Unfortunately, such a theory would present an unprecedented challenge. Quantum theory postulates that by the act of observing an experiment the results are affected. Yet observation is the current cornerstone of scientific inquiry. He wrote in *A Briefer History of Time*, "Yet if there really were a complete unified theory, it would also determine our actions—so the theory itself would determine the outcome of our search for it."

Arguably, Hawking echoes this concern at a higher level of understanding than enjoyed by any other living person, so there is little hope for you and me of drawing any further useful conclusions, other than remaining open to new possibilities.

It does not seem as if an answer to these questions is likely to surface soon; however, Wilkinson has found these ideas helpful, as have others. Einstein believed that events that seemingly defy the laws of probability will one day be explained. In one of his letters to the physicist Max Born in 1947, he wrote that he thinks he had a continuous-field theory that avoids "spooky action at a distance,"[9] and that in the future a theory that does not depend on probabilities will be developed.

I'll finish with an interesting little snippet that I saw in the *Metro* newspaper in 2010.[10] It concerns the successful collision of two subatomic particles at the speed of light in the Large Hadron Collider.

"There are known unknowns out there, like dark matter and new dimensions about which we hope to learn," said CERN research director Sergio Bertolucci. "But it is possible we will find some unknown unknowns which could be hugely important for mankind."

I found these comments rather frightening. My fears increased during 2011 when scientists discovered that neutrinos travel faster than the speed of light, which is impossible if the law of relativity is to be believed. Worse was to come a few months later, when the scientists checked their calculations again and found that they had put the decimal point in the wrong place or something.

These are the same people who collide subatomic particles at the speed of light, relying on unknown unknowns. By comparison, you and I are the most sensible people on the planet.

Now review your notes and thoughts on this chapter.

Ask yourself this question: "What three things can I do now that can help me immediately, or at least in the very near future, to make more luck and find more health, wealth, and happiness?"

Write your three points down in the booth.

The next chapter is also the final one. I warn my clients as they start their online course or attend my workshops that they are on a journey. It is a journey that will take many unexpected turns and at times will appear bewilderingly complicated.

However, the final steps are perhaps the easiest, with the dawning realization that there are a lot fewer changes to make in our strategies and processes than we imagined. So now it is time to digest the nuggets from these final steps.

Meditation Booth
Three Nuggets for Now

1.

2.

3.

Conclusion

What Next?

This book is deliberately not just a list of recommendations designed to make you luckier and more mindful and to produce more flow in your life. The most important ingredient in your search for more luck and the health, wealth, and happiness that follow luck will not be what has been written. It will, instead, be your own thoughts that surface, as if from nowhere, and guide you toward what instinctively feels like the right direction.

My efforts have been limited to attempt to engage with your unconscious mind, plant a few ideas, and put you in touch with the resources that will lead you toward wherever your luck hides, and hence to the success, health, wealth, and happiness that lies beyond.

What works for you may not for another person, and vice versa. But the following are more likely:

- If you read the whole of this book, it is possible you will find more luck.
- If you also write down the key nuggets and your three action points at the end of each chapter, it is probable you will find more luck.
- If you also remind yourself daily about your three action points at the end of each chapter, it is almost certain that you will find more luck.
- If you also tell another person about your three action points at the end of each chapter, it is guaranteed that you will find more luck.

Run with the Ball

There is something else you may choose to do, and it will be very powerful. Many successful business leaders have just one piece of paper on their desk, and they review it each morning. This paper is the distilled life essence of their empire. It comprises the few key critical factors that define success or failure. All are measurable, and the CEO is only happy when he has his or her finger on this pulse.

You, too, will benefit from a similar approach. Cut and paste all of your chapter nuggets onto one piece of paper. Review this list every morning and pick five items to take action on that day. Review it again at the end of each day and record your score.

Even if you did not hit all of your targets, you will still feel happier than you might expect. This is because you have exercised a degree of control over your life, and that is something we all want more of.

Another suggestion for your consideration is to use this one page as the front cover of your own book of life. This book would be an informal scrapbook of all the things that are most important to you. These pictures and notes would include your family and friends, your successes, and your dreams for the future. Your scrapbook would also include all the different ways you will continue to reinvent yourself and acquire new skills and knowledge.

One of the few things that I learned during an expensive business-training course was that in today's rapidly changing world it is necessary to replace 25 percent of your intellectual content each year just to stand still.

In the preceding chapters, I have written many times about the miracles within our body. I am not convinced that Darwin's laws of natural selection are sufficient explanation for their brilliance, but it is the best scientific model that we have at the moment. I certainly keep an open mind about divine creation, too. The truth is that I do not know, but it does not matter.

One lucky spin-off from my Darwinian interest was the opportunity to play him in an international television documentary series. Even luckier was the opportunity to sit in his chair while filming, handle his manuscripts and specimens, and imagine seeing the world through his eyes.

Our view of the universe is limited, even though each generation uncovers a new level of complexity and moves to a higher degree of understanding. Just when we think we know all the answers, some crazy scientist discovers something new that turns our comfortable view of the world upside down.

Powerful telescopes reveal new galaxies; electron microscopes reveal new structures, too, but in the cells of our bodies, structures that had remained hidden from view since these cells were first seen by the earliest microscopes in the mid-seventeenth century.

In both examples, much of what we do see is empty space, but I cannot help thinking that it is not empty. It just appears so to our narrow and feeble vision. Whatever fills this space may one day be an explanation for the many things that we cannot currently explain.

Fortunately, we do not need explanations to find luck. Our role is just to keep looking and allow the future to take care of itself.

Remember the newborn baby I mentioned in the introduction? It was 99.99 percent complete, lacking only a conscious mind. Years later, it has completed its development. Its conscious mind is now firmly in control and has conveniently forgotten that it still only forms 0.01 percent of its existence.

This conscious mind was shaped as a result of life experiences and in response to interactions with other people. Some of these experiences would have been positive and others far less so. The degree of resultant happiness depends less on the pleasure associated with these experiences than on how this person chooses to think about them.

How many open doors were explored during its life, and how many remained unseen or unopened, with the result that the riches beyond were lost forever? Did this person move forward with life and find happiness, or move backward? Was the world a better place for its life or for its passing?

Just thinking about these things is likely to enrich your life, and your life is all that matters. It is the only life that you can control, even if only just a little. And a little bit more control can make all the difference.

I sincerely hope that you have found at least one idea within this book that will lead you to attracting at least a few more lucky breaks. Perhaps you found many. Either way, I would like to know. How did it change your life? What value did it hold? Were you surprised, or did you sense that it was waiting for you?

I know from discussing luck and related concepts with thousands of clients and delegates that some skills are acquired much easier through sensory channels other than only the written word. I have highlighted some of these in earlier chapters, and they include goals, the three Hs of havening, HeartMath, and hypnosis, and the most interesting of them all, the subject of magic, a subject that children may understand better than we do. These subjects form the foundation of my workshop and online coaching courses, and have produced magical and sometimes very rapid results.

Please feel free to write to me with your comments through my website, drstephensimpson.com. If you have a question, I will do my best to answer that, too, either personally or through my blog. Sign up for the blogs and newsletter; they are free and full of tips, insights from other readers, and sometimes free offers, too. Even better, write a short article, and I'll do my best to publish it.

Remember, the only limits are those that you set yourself or that others impose upon you. Whichever route you take, I wish you a pleasant journey. I hope that the success, health, wealth, and happiness you find at your destination exceeds your wildest expectations.

Safe travels.

About the Author

Dr. Stephen Simpson is a fellow of the Royal Society of Medicine and an elite performance director. He regularly appears on TV and radio, and his clients include leading names from the diverse worlds of sports, business, the entertainment industries, and professional poker.

Dr. Simpson is also a best-selling author, actor, and presenter, as well as a feature writer for *The Best You* magazine. His articles appear regularly in leading newspapers and magazines.

Details of these articles, audiobooks, books, podcasts, and videos can be found on the website drstephensimpson.com.

NOTES

1. http://www.drstephensimpson.com/home/2014/11

2. Scotland Institute of Sport, Understanding Talent: Mindset, *British Swimming Coaches Association,* accessed November 7, 2015, http://www.gbswimcoaches.co.uk/wp-content/uploads/2012/05/Mindset-Presentation-GB-Coaching-Workshop-2011.pdf.

3. Hirini Reedy, "Mental Toughness for Modern Life," *International Mental Game Coaching Association*, accessed November 7, 2015, http://www.mentalgamecoaching.com/IMGCAArticles/MentalToughness/MentalToughness.html.

4. "Havening Techniques," accessed November 7, 2015, http://www.havening.org.

5. "Expanding Heart Connections," *HeartMath Institute*, accessed November 7, 2015, https://www.heartmath.org.

6. HeartMath Research Center, "Science of the Heart, *Institute of Heart Math*, accessed November 7, 2015, https://www.heartmath.org/assets/uploads/2015/01/science-of-the-heart.pdf.

7. "Technical Report: Hypnosis in Action," *The Black Vault*, accessed November 7, 2015, http://documents.theblackvault.com/documents/mindcontrol/hypnosisinintelligence.pdf.

8. Gottfried J. Mayer-Kress, "Complex Systems as Fundamental Theory of Sports Coaching?" *Cornell University Library*, accessed November 7, 2015, http://arxiv.org/html/nlin/0111009.

9. "Einstein's 'Spooky Action at a Distance' Paradox Older than Thought," *MIT Technology Review*, March 8, 2012, http://www.technologyreview.

com/view/427174/einsteins-spooky-action-at-a-distance-paradox-older-than-thought/.

10. "Large Hadron Collider to Give Answer to Universe's 'Known Unknowns,'" *Metro*, March 30, 2010, http://metro.co.uk/2010/03/30/large-hadron-collider-to-give-answers-to-universes-known-unknowns-203154/.

Made in the USA
Charleston, SC
16 September 2016